"Compulsively
inviting . . . irresistible."
—*INDEPENDENT*

"Intriguing . . . satisfyingly
replete with eye-popping stories."
—*OBSERVER*

"Fascinating . . . beautifully made."
—*IT'S NICE THAT*

"Vivid and haunting."
—*PEAK ADVERTISER*

"Poignant . . . a great story
told by a great writer."
—*KENT ON SUNDAY*

"A fascinating read."
—*PRE-RAPHAELITE
SISTERHOOD*

"Illuminating."
—*KIRKUS REVIEWS*

"Bold and insightful."
—*ROYALTY*

"Densely researched,
clearly written."
—*THE LADY* MAGAZINE

"A fluid, contemporary classic."
—*SKY*

"Strong."
—*LIBRARY JOURNAL*

"Highly original and
beautifully illustrated."
—*TOWN DAILY*

"Irresistible."
—*LONDON SUNDAY TIMES*

"Entertaining and . . . vivid insight."
—UK PRESS SYNDICATION

"Lively, engaging, and
buoyantly enthusiastic."
—*LONDON SUNDAY TIMES*

"Rare insight."
—*WESTERN GAZETTE*

"Well worth writing . . .
well worth reading."
—*LONDON SUNDAY TIMES*

"Engaging prose . . .
[a] handsome book."
—*WORLD OF
INTERIORS*

"Mesmerising . . . and gripping."
—*MAIL ON SUNDAY*

Victorian Christmas

Victorian Christmas

Traditional Recipes, Decorations, Activities, and Carols

Lucinda Dickens Hawksley

Countryman Press

An Imprint of W. W. Norton & Company
Independent Publishers Since 1923

For information about permission to reproduce selections
from this book, write to Permissions, Countryman Press,
500 Fifth Avenue, New York, NY 10110

For information about special discounts for bulk purchases,
please contact W. W. Norton Special Sales at
specialsales@wwnorton.com or 800-233-4830

Manufacturing by RRD Asia
Book design by Allison Chi
Production manager: Devon Zahn

Countryman Press
www.countrymanpress.com

An imprint of W. W. Norton & Company, Inc.
500 Fifth Avenue, New York, NY 10110
www.wwnorton.com

978-1-68268-863-2

10 9 8 7 6 5 4 3 2 1

For D
with love

Contents

Portrait of Charles Dickens by
Margaret Gillies, painted in 1843 as he was
writing *A Christmas Carol*

Introduction

W hen I was young, my parents made Christmas a wonderful time of celebrating with family and friends, playing classic festive games, such as charades, and encouraging my sisters and me to write and perform plays for my grandparents—just as, I later discovered, Charles and Catherine Dickens did with their children. In the days before television and the Internet, how else would they have amused *ten* children? Many of the seasonal events that my family enjoys today—including an annual reading of my great-great-great-grandfather's iconic novella *A Christmas Carol* and, whenever possible, celebrating all twelve days of Christmas, ending with a party on Twelfth Night—began with previous generations.

To me, the 6th of January always seemed one of the saddest days of the year: The Christmas decorations come down, and for those of us in the Northern Hemisphere, sparkling lights no longer relieve the gloom of long, dark, cold winter nights. A few years ago, I lived and worked in Guatemala, where I learned that Guatemalans keep their Christmas lights up until Candlemas (the 2nd of

February), a tradition I happily adopted. The point of the festive season is to enjoy the holiday in your own way, making the most of what delights you and your loved ones. If Victorian history and traditions interest you, I hope that this book helps to make your own Christmas as festive as possible, by describing entertaining customs of our ancestors, and that it helps you create new traditions to pass to future generations.

Many myths and legends have grown up around Christmas. Different countries observe the holiday differently, but all who celebrate it share numerous beliefs and practices. The Victorians, in their time of reform and radical change, keenly understood that they risked losing the customs of the past. They enjoyed reviving those earlier traditions and, in their own time, originated many new customs that we still follow today. This book celebrates the ways in which they observed Christmas and the resonances that those traditions still carry today.

A SHORT HISTORY OF CHRISTMAS TO 1837

In the New Testament, the Gospels of Matthew and Luke, both written around AD 80, contain brief narratives describing the birth of Jesus Christ. Early records indicate that believers were celebrating the occasion in the AD 100s.

According to tradition, St. Lucia—one of those early believers and another great name associated with the holiday season—was born in Syracuse, Sicily, in 283. Various biographies, written over the course of a thousand years, give different accounts of her life. In all of them, a jilted fiancé or suitor reported her for the crime of being a Christian, and authorities executed her in 304. Western Christianity celebrates her feast day on the 13th of December, which in some countries marks the beginning of the holiday season. Her name comes from *lux*, Latin for "light," and observances of her martyrdom emphasise candles as a symbol of the light of hope piercing darkness, echoing earlier pagan festivals associated with midwinter. Scandinavians, for example, celebrate the day with parades in which children, dressed in white robes and with evergreen wreaths on their heads, hold candles as they walk.

The most important saint associated with Christmas is St. Nicholas, of course, but there's more than one with the same name! According to tradition, the man who became the saint now revered for giving timely gifts was born around 260 on the southern coast of current-day Türkiye. One account holds that—when he heard about three young women from a family so poor that their father was planning to sell them into prostitution to prevent them from dying of starvation—Nicholas secretly gave the family small bags of gold coins. Over time the story evolved, making the home so difficult to enter that he tossed the bags down the chimney. The gold landed in the young women's stockings, which they had hung by the fireplace to dry. From that narrative comes the Christmas tradition of hanging stockings by a fireplace. The feast day of St. Nicholas takes place on the 6th of December.

In the Roman Empire, the 25th of March marked the vernal equinox—celebrated in the Church as the Feast of the Annunciation, meaning the conception of Jesus Christ—and nine months later comes the 25th of December, the date of the winter solstice on the Julian calendar. Romans celebrated the old pagan festival of Saturnalia roughly from the 17th to the 23rd of December, so the new holy day aligned easily with existing observances. The first recorded Christmas celebration took place in Rome on the 25th of December 336, and Christianity became the official religion of the Roman Empire in 380. For early Christians, the Christmas season lasted 40 days, until Candlemas, also called the Feast of the

Presentation of Jesus Christ or the Feast of the Purification of the Blessed Virgin Mary.

Christians in different parts of the world, however, observe Christmas on different days. In some countries, the celebration falls on the 24th of December; in others on the 25th of December. Many Orthodox Christians celebrate Christmas Day on the 6th of January, yet that same day, for others, serves as Christmas Eve. For Western Christianity, the 6th of January marks the Feast of the Epiphany, also called Three Kings Day. In 567, the Council of Tours formally organised the Christmas season in the West, establishing Advent as the time of preparation for Christmas and the 12 days from Christmas to Epiphany as a sacred, festive period. In medieval Europe, many Christians also observed Candlemas as the end of the holiday season.

In the early Middle Ages, the prominence of Christmas slowly declined in favour of celebrating Epiphany. In 800, however, following the tradition established by Byzantine emperors, Pope Leo III crowned Charlemagne as emperor of the Holy Roman Empire on the 25th of December. In 1066, the archbishop of York crowned King William I of England on the same day. Not long after, the word *Christmas* first occurs in Old English, appearing as the phrase *Xres maesse* in *The Anglo-Saxon Chronicle*, written around 1100. In Old English, *Xres* equates to the modern *Xmas*, proving, contrary to popular belief, that Xmas isn't a modern abbreviation. *Cristes maesse*, meaning "Christ's mass," refers to the liturgical service celebrating the birth of Jesus Christ. The *Xr* in Xres and the *X* in Xmas come from the spelling of *Christ* in ancient Greek: Χριστός (*Christós*), which means "anointed." In English, the phrase *Cristes maesse* became one word in the 1300s.

The first mention of a man symbolising the holiday comes from the next century. Written in the mid-1400s, "Sir Christemas," a short carol attributed to Richard Smart, a rector in Devon, England, includes the call-and-response dialogue:

"I am here, Sir Christemas."
"Welcome, my lord Christemas."

In 1616, King James VI of Scotland / I of England and Ireland commissioned playwright and poet Ben Jonson to write a festive play for the English court. In Jonson's *Christmas: His Masque*, Old Gregorie Christmas personifies the holiday, wearing "long Stockings, a close Doublet, a high crown'd Hat with a Broach, a long thin beard, a Truncheon, little Ruffes, white Shoes, his Scarffes, and Garters tyed crosse." Old Gregorie Christmas's fittingly named children also appear, including Carol, Mince Pie, Mumming, New Yeare's Gift, and Wassail. In the 1600s, as the colony of New Amsterdam (now New York City) grew, Dutch settlers brought with them the observance of St. Nicholas's feast day. Sint Nikolaas, his name in Dutch, evolved into Sinterklaas, from which the name Santa Claus comes. When German settlers arrived in North America, they spoke of *das Christkindl*, the Christ child, which English speakers anglicised to Kris Kringle, another name for the figure of Christmas.

But it wasn't all smooth sailing for the holiday. Over the centuries, various reformers tried to change the Catholic Church. In reaction to clerical excess and corruption, Protestantism gained significant popularity in the 1500s. Following in the footsteps of the English Reformation, the Scottish Reformation led to the creation of the Church of Scotland, a Calvinist Presbyterian faith that considered Christmas much too Catholic. The Scottish Church banned Christmas in 1573, abolishing "all days that hereto have been kept holy except the Sabbath day, such as Yule day, saints days, and such others." Many Scots defied the ban, though, so religious leaders in Scotland declared war on the holiday, virulently trying to erase the occasion. Church officials prohibited special Christmas services, singing carols, and other holiday celebrations. They even forbade bakers from making Christmas foods and compelled them to report anyone who dared order mince pies, Yule bread, and other traditional delicacies.

The 1600s also spelled trouble for Christmas. A new religious fervour was sweeping across northern Europe. Adherents to Puritanism, a fundamentalist sect of Christianity that also condemned Catholicism, set their sights on other Protestant denominations, all "ungodly" in their view. The Bible didn't mention celebrating Christmas, so the Puritans argued that no one should, especially because traditional festivities often involved raucous feasting, drinking, and debauchery. In Scotland, so many people disregarded the religious prohibition that Scottish Parliament entered the fray, outlawing the holiday in 1640. Even after the repeal of that ban, Hogmanay—Scottish New Year's Eve—still remains more popular than Christmas.

Meanwhile, in England, a civil war was brewing. Royalists, called Cavaliers, backed King Charles I, while Parliamentarians, known as Roundheads, who ultimately won the bloody conflict, backed Oliver Cromwell, a Puritan. Just like the Presbyterians to their north, the Puritans railed against Christmas, banning it in England in 1647. This injunction extended beyond religious services to include decorating homes with mistletoe, wreaths, and yule logs, all denounced as pagan, and making special foods for the occasion. Later laws even established fines for holding or attending Christmas services.

Just as the Scots had done, the broader English public resisted the legislation. "The World Turn'd Upside Down," a popular ballad, jibed:

Command is given. We must obey
and quite forget old Christmas day.

In 1652, John Taylor, a Thames boatman furious about the ban, wrote "The Vindication of Christmas," a pamphlet defending the people's right to celebrate Christmas with traditional activities and food: roasting apples, playing cards, singing carols, dancing, and more. In the illustration on the cover, Old Christmas—dressed in a fashionable hat and long robes, sporting long hair and a long beard—says to a Puritan, "O Sir I bring good cheere." The sword-carrying Puritan replies: "Keep out." In the anonymous pamphlets of this time, the personification of Christmas takes on the title of "Father."

In 1660, the parliaments of England and Scotland restored their monarchies, calling back King Charles II, who sat on both thrones. The king dissolved the bans on Christmas, but the war against the holiday continued with the Puritans who sailed to America to escape the perceived impurity of Europe. In 1659, John Endecott, governor of the Massachusetts Bay Colony, also banned Christmas. That ban remained in place until Governor Simon Bradstreet overturned it in 1681. New Englanders, like the Scots, didn't embrace Christmas again fully until the Victorian era.

Elsewhere, colonial Americans celebrated Christmas without limitations. Moravians in the Pennsylvania Dutch communities of Bethlehem and Nazareth and in the Wachovia tract of North Carolina observed it enthusiastically. The Moravian community of Bethlehem introduced Christmas trees and nativity scenes to America. But most Americans didn't make much of the holiday, a key reason that General George Washington attacked the British Army's Hessian mercenaries on the 26th of December 1776 in the Battle of Trenton. Before the battle, one of Washington's officers noted that "they make a great deal of Christmas in Germany." After the War of Independence, celebrating Christmas, seen as more of a British custom, declined among Americans whose families hailed from the British Isles. But the tradition remained strong among Americans not of British heritage, such as the Dutch, Germans, and others.

In 1809, the people of New York City read a series of newspaper advertisements concerning the whereabouts of Diedrich Knickerbocker, a Dutch historian. Everyone was talking about the man, unaware that he didn't exist. Author Washington Irving had orchestrated the ruse to publicise his new book, *A History of New York*. Written from Knickerbocker's perspective, the book offered a witty, deliberately flawed chronicle of New York under Dutch rule in the 1600s. In one story, a Dutch crew survives a shipwreck and comes ashore in Manhattan, where one of the sailors sees "good St. Nicholas . . . riding over the tops of the trees, in that self-same wagon wherein he brings his yearly presents to children." Irving adored the legend of St. Nicholas and wrote several Christmas stories, most notably *Old Christmas* and *The Keeping of Christmas at Bracebridge Hall*. In 1835, he also organised the Saint Nicholas

"There is something in the very season of the year that gives a charm to the festivity of Christmas. At other times, we derive a great portion of our pleasures from the mere beauties of nature. . . . But in the depth of winter . . . we feel more sensibly the charm of each other's society and are brought more closely together by dependence on each other for enjoyment. . . . The pitchy gloom without makes the heart dilate on entering the room filled with the glow and warmth of the evening fire. . . . The English . . . have always been fond of those festivals and holidays . . . and social rites of Christmas. . . . The old halls of castles and manor-houses resounded with the harp and the Christmas carol, and their ample boards groaned under the weight of hospitality. Even the poorest cottage welcomed the festive season with green decorations of bay and holly."

—From *The Keeping of Christmas at Bracebridge Hall* by Washington Irving, 1822

Society of the City of New York to preserve and promote the city's Dutch heritage.

While Irving was popularising Christmas, Arthur Stansbury, another New Yorker and a Presbyterian minister, wrote *The Children's Friend: A New-Year's Present to the Little Ones from Five to Twelve*, a long poem that includes the lines

> Old Santeclaus, with much delight,
> His reindeer drives this frosty night,
> O'er chimney tops and tracks of snow,
> To bring his yearly gifts to you.

When published, the poem contained the first known illustration of Santa Claus.

Meanwhile, back in Britain, some members of the Church of England were placing a renewed emphasis on the religious observance of Christmas. They soon established the Oxford Movement, which sought to revive certain Catholic traditions in the Anglican faith. In December 1833, the writing career of my ancestor Charles Dickens began when the *Monthly Magazine* published his short story "A Dinner at Poplar Walk." Two years later, he wrote "Christmas Festivities," a short character piece renamed "A Christmas Dinner" when collected in 1836 with other short stories in the book *Sketches by Boz*.

In June 1837, King William IV died. His niece and heir presumptive, 18-year-old Princess Alexandrina Victoria, became queen, ushering in the Victorian era. Her reign encompassed more than six decades, which witnessed great reforms, advancements, upheavals, and conquests. During that time, much of the world changed, including how people celebrated Christmas.

The Coronation of Queen Victoria by Edmund Parris

State Portrait of HM Queen Victoria 1838 by George Hayter

CHRISTMAS IN THE VICTORIAN ERA

At the dawn of the 1800s, only the wealthy and privileged enjoyed Christmas in the way that most of us imagine a Victorian Christmas. For many working people, the 24th and 25th of December functioned as working days like any others. For those in domestic service, Christmas meant working even harder than usual to ensure that employers had a special festive season. That workload left servants little time to enjoy themselves. As the century progressed, however, the occasion became more egalitarian as social expectations prompted employers to grant staff a proper holiday. The Industrial Revolution and continued technological innovation in the 1800s increased economic prosperity, amplifying the number of people able to observe the occasion. As the middle classes expanded, more people than in previous centuries could afford to celebrate the holiday in style.

Nevertheless, in the early Victorian era, many felt that Christmas had lost its meaning. Newspaper journalists lamented that it had become "too commercial" and that the public largely had forgotten the holiday tradition of giving charity and help to those in need. Charles Dickens had a plan, however. He marshalled the power of his pen to inspire positive change. Following the publication of *A Christmas Carol* in 1843, Christmas underwent a dramatic renaissance not only in Britain but also overseas. Christmas and its charitable connotations suddenly became fashionable again. The transformation of Ebenezer Scrooge from miser to philanthropist restored what many considered the true meaning of the occasion.

In America, the legacy of Puritanism had suppressed meaningful observance of the holiday, particularly in the Northeast. But by 1856, the tide was turning. In April of that year, the General Court

"Who can be insensible to the outpourings of good feeling, and the honest interchange of affectionate attachment, which abound at this season of the year? A Christmas family-party! We know nothing in nature more delightful! There seems a magic in the very name of Christmas. Petty jealousies and discords are forgotten; social feelings are awakened, in bosoms to which they have long been strangers; father and son, or brother and sister, who have met and passed with averted gaze, or a look of cold recognition, for months before, proffer and return the cordial embrace, and bury their past animosities in their present happiness. Kindly hearts that have yearned towards each other, but have been withheld by false notions of pride and self-dignity, are again reunited, and all is kindness and benevolence! Would that Christmas lasted the whole year through (as it ought)."

—From "A Christmas Dinner"
by Charles Dickens, 1836

of Massachusetts made Christmas an official holiday in the Bay State. On that first legal Christmas in more than 200 years, poet Henry Longfellow recorded in his journal, "We are in a transition state about Christmas here in New England. The old Puritan feeling prevents it from being a cheerful, hearty holiday; though every year makes it more so." By 1860, almost half of the states in the Union had declared the occasion a legal holiday. In 1870, the federal government declared Christmas a national holiday, and the next year Scotland followed suit, establishing it as a bank holiday. Elsewhere in Britain and Ireland, people considered Christmas Day a traditional day of rest, the same as Sunday, but that convention didn't preclude many people from having to work. The Bank Holidays Act of 1871, however, did establish a holiday for Boxing Day, the 26th of December, particularly important for those in domestic service.

Let's take a closer look at how the Victorians marked the occasion with food and drink, decorations, activities, and carols.

A Note on the Text

This book treads an unusual textual path. I'm British, my publisher is American, and this book is for readers of English all over the world. One text can't accommodate all the variations of spelling, punctuation, and other conventions in all countries. With that in mind and attentive to the topic at hand, the text uses British spellings and dates with American punctuation and provides both imperial and metric measures.

Food
&
Drink

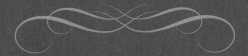

"It was the day before Christmas; such a cold east wind! such an inky sky! such a blue-black look in people's faces, as they were driven out more than usual, to complete their purchases for the next day's festival.

Before leaving home that morning, Jenkins had given some money to his wife to buy the next day's dinner.

'My dear, I wish for turkey and sausages. It may be a weakness, but I own I am partial to sausages. My deceased mother was. Such tastes are hereditary. As to the sweets— whether plum-pudding or mince-pies—I leave such considerations to you; I only beg you not to mind expense. Christmas comes but once a year.'"

—From "Christmas Storms and Sunshine"
by Elizabeth Gaskell, 1848

F ROM THE earliest days of celebrating Christmas, food has served as a focal point of the festivities. When Puritans came to power in England in 1647, they forbade traditional Christmas foods. With the restoration of the monarchy in 1660, England resumed sumptuous feasting for the occasion. Many of the holiday foods that we consider traditional, however, only became popular in the Victorian age.

In the 1800s, European empires forged trade routes across the world, increasing the variety of foods available in markets and shops. At the same time, magazines and cookbooks became more affordable and available, feeding a growing interest in cooking across the social scale. For Christmas, those who could afford it chose from a dizzying array of meats and poultry: beef, mutton, pork, turkey, goose, and game birds, all served at the same meal. For people of means, Christmas, like any other occasion, had to demonstrate societal standing and luxury. Their seasonal feasts incorporated ingredients not easily obtained, such as wine and brandy from France, oranges from Spain, Port from Portugal, lemons from Italy, and various spices and dried fruits from far-off lands. Many Christmas recipes deliberately used these hard-to-source foods to establish social status amid the importance of the religious occasion.

CHRISTMAS DINNER

Published first in instalments and then as a book in 1758, *The British Housewife, or the Cook, Housekeeper's and Gardiner's Companion* by Martha Bradley gave advice about foods available, month by month. For December, "Butcher's Meat in general is never in better season than at this Time of Year, and Beef in particular may appear in the largest Pieces at the best Tables: the French Fashions have carried it a great way against us, but they have not arrived yet so far as to banish the Sirloin of Beef from a Christmas dinner."

Almost a century later, the royal family's Christmas dinner still followed that tradition. From 1840 to 1842, Charles Francatelli served as head chef for Queen Victoria. On the 31st of December 1843, *The Planet*, a London newspaper, reported on the queen's Christmas feast at Windsor Castle:

> Her Majesty and Prince Albert, with the whole of the household, attended Divine Service in the private chapel within the Castle. In the afternoon, Prince Albert drove her Majesty out in a pony phaeton. The banquet in the evening took place in the grand dining room. The chief dish was a baron of beef, nearly four feet long, and between two and three feet in width, and weighing 180lbs. There was like-wise placed upon one of the side tables the hump of the Brahmin ox, pre-sented to her Majesty by Viscount Combermere, and slaughtered at the Royal dairy. . . . There were, like-wise, on the banquet table, several turkeys, peahens, and Cochin China pullets, which had been reared and fattened at the Royal aviary in the Home Park.

After leaving the queen's household, Francatelli wrote his first cookbook, *The Modern Cook*, published in 1846. That record offers valuable insight into how he prepared the dishes served to the queen and her family.

For most people, though, the holiday meal had changed dra-matically. Poultry—first goose, then turkey—largely took pride of place on the Victorian Christmas table. Tradition called for goose because families of moderate means could rear geese easily, eat-ing their eggs regularly and only occasionally slaughtering one for meat. After the Industrial Revolution, which took place roughly

VICTORIAN CHRISTMAS

from 1760 to 1850, huge swathes of the rural population left the countryside to work and live in cities, where keeping geese proved less easy. But even as late as 1892, plenty of people still ate goose for the holiday. In the Sherlock Holmes story "The Adventure of the Blue Carbuncle," published in January of that year, Arthur Conan Doyle wrote about a Christmas goose club. In this popular Victorian scheme, people with limited income gave, in the months leading to Christmas, a small amount from their weekly wages to a grocer or pub owner. When they had saved enough, they received a goose to take home to their family.

In current-day Mexico, Indigenous people domesticated the turkey long before Europeans arrived. The Spanish brought turkeys to Europe around 1520, and merchants brought the birds to England roughly by 1540. Because of their rarity, only the very wealthy ate turkey at this time. The archives of the Worshipful Company of Poulters of London show that, at the end of the 1600s, company clerks each received a turkey as a Christmas gift. Most people outside that trade guild wouldn't have eaten turkey at any time of the year, making it an exclusive present.

In the mid-1800s, when the legacy of the bird as a wealthy delicacy met advances in domestic poultry farming, eating turkey for Christmas became popular in Britain. In *A Christmas Carol*, Ebenezer Scrooge buys one for the Cratchit family. Readers of the time would have recognised that expensive gesture as an unusual offering for a poor family. In 1861, Isabella Beeton, author of *Mrs. Beeton's Book of Household Management*, recorded seeing turkeys being walked more than 100 miles from Norfolk to London for sale in Christmas markets. By the time Queen Victoria died in 1901, turkey had become an accepted part of the British Christmas feast. For those who couldn't afford to buy meat or fowl,

Bronze turkeys from the *Cyclopedia of Live Stock*, 1881

however, Christmas dinner consisted of whatever they could catch or scrounge for the pot.

Feeding the Poor

Nineteenth-century newspapers contain many references to feeding the poor with festive Christmas dinners and parties. Written from and for the perspective of well-off readers, the reporting applauds those involved for one act of charitable kindness on a single day of the year. The articles never suggest that anyone might consult the poor about their needs and seemed unconcerned that, after that single grand meal, those living in poverty had to fend for themselves once more.

A Christmas Carol details the impoverished Cratchit family's Christmas dinner and its meagre amounts of food:

> Bob said he didn't believe there ever was such a goose cooked. Its tenderness and flavour, size and cheapness, were the themes of universal admiration. Eked out by apple-sauce and mashed potatoes, it was a sufficient dinner for the whole family; indeed, as Mrs. Cratchit said with great delight (surveying one small atom of a bone upon the dish), they hadn't ate it all at last! Yet every one had had enough, and the youngest Cratchits in particular, were steeped in sage and onion to the eyebrows! . . . In half a minute, Mrs Cratchit entered: flushed, but smiling proudly: with the pudding, like a speckled cannon-ball, so hard and firm, blazing in half of half-a-quartern of ignited brandy, and bedight with Christmas holly stuck into the top.

Victorian Vegetables

In the 1200s, farmers in current-day Belgium began cultivating the humble Brussels sprout as we know it. It took a long time, however, for this miniature cabbage to spread to the rest of the world. The French brought it to Louisiana in the 1700s, and Brussels sprouts reached Britain in the early 1800s. A hardy vegetable, it grows well in cold-weather climates, making it a popular produce for winter in general and Christmas in particular.

Not all Victorians ate meat for Christmas dinner. In the 1800s, an awareness of the need for healthier eating grew, and social reformers eagerly promoted vegetarianism. A week before Christmas 1899, the editor of the *Carmarthen Weekly Reporter*, a newspaper in

Brussels Sprouts

southwestern Wales, published this letter from G. C. Wade, provisional secretary of the Vegetarian Federal Union:

> Christmas is near, and I would fain ask if it is in accordance with our boasted civilization and our *fin de siècle* refinement to continue to make it a fetish of slaughter and guzzle, going to church or chapel and shouting, "Christians, awake! Salute the happy morn," and then making a holocaust of innocent animals, and a financial boom to brewers, butchers, and publicans, with a resulting benefit to purveyors of patent pills and undertakers? There will, of course, be feasts given to the poor, and rightly so; but why must it always be the boorish diet of "beef and swipes"? Why, sir, three times the number could be fed for the same money on a judicious temperance and vegetarian diet. . . . Is it not, therefore, wiser to feed three times the number on a rational, harmless diet, instead of only a few, on a stimulating, disease-producing one, creating, may be, a taste that many can never afford to gratify afterwards?

Christmas Sweets

Familiar to many and initially a savoury dish, mince pies originally consisted of minced meat, as the name suggests, baked in a pastry crust. Over the centuries, however, the recipe evolved. As the British Empire expanded, importers introduced many new ingredients from all over the world to British and American tables, and cooks prided themselves on modernising their mincemeat recipes to include these new delicacies. By the Victorian era, the pies had become sweet: The meat had dwindled to just lard in the crust and suet to bind the dried fruit, nuts, and sugar.

Christmas Pudding

"The Plum pudding is a national symbol. It does not represent a class or caste but the bulk of the English nation."
—From the *Illustrated London News*, 1850

The tale of Christmas pudding begins with frumenty, an ancient porridge made with wheat cooked in milk or a meat broth and sometimes modified with currants, almonds, or even saffron. As you can imagine, versions of that simple, nourishing dish exist in many cuisines all over the world. In English, the first known recipe dates to the late 1300s. Dried fruit entered the recipe in the 1700s, which turned frumenty into a type of fig or plum pudding, the precursor to Christmas pudding. By the 1800s, it had become a dessert rather than an accompaniment to meat, as in the past. In its sweet incarnation, cracked wheat is boiled in water, milk, or cream; eggs, salt, sugar, and sometimes saffron join the mixture; and it is baked until thick.

In the 1830s, recipes appeared for what we recognise as Christmas pudding today: a boiled cake made from flour, fruit, spices,

Mother and son stirring Christmas pudding from *The Mothers' Companion*, 1895

sugar, and suet. Then, in 1845, Longmans published *Modern Cookery for Private Families* by Eliza Acton. Her book featured discrete lists of ingredients, specific measures, and cooking times. It also included the first recipe named Christmas Pudding (page 38). Once famous in the world of cookery, Acton's name remains little

"Oh, a wonderful pudding! Bob Cratchit said, and calmly too, that he regarded it as the greatest success achieved by Mrs. Cratchit since their marriage. Mrs. Cratchit said that now the weight was off her mind, she would confess she had had her doubts about the quantity of flour. Everybody had something to say about it, but nobody said or thought it was at all a small pudding for a large family. It would have been flat heresy to do so. Any Cratchit would have blushed to hint at such a thing."

—From *A Christmas Carol*
by **Charles Dickens, 1843**

remembered today, eclipsed by others who followed in her footsteps, but her work offered a lifeline for many Victorian women. An intelligent young woman, Acton began her writing career as a poet before Longmans asked her to produce the cookbook. An instant hit, it sold more than 60,000 copies in 40 editions. Her writing showed a charming sense of humour, with recipe titles such as The Poor Author's Pudding, made from frugal ingredients, and The Publisher's Pudding, containing cream and Cognac. Acton died in 1859, two years before Samuel Beeton published his wife's famous cookbook, which contained many of Acton's recipes.

As with many Victorian customs, Christmas pudding reshaped an older tradition. From at least the late 1700s and probably earlier, Stir-Up Sunday marked the occasion, on the fifth Sunday before Christmas, for preparing mincemeat. The name comes from a line in the *Book of Common Prayer*: "Stir up, we beseech thee, O Lord, the wills of thy faithful people." As Christmas pudding grew more popular, however, the tradition shifted to making the all-important boiled confection, gathering family for a new ceremony built on an older one. Every family member—and, in wealthy houses, the staff—stirred the pudding from east to west, commemorating the journey of the Magi to the newborn Jesus. The new tradition also reportedly brought luck to the family, and everyone who stirred was expected to make a silent wish.

Candy Canes

Before manufacturers invented reusable decorations—such as glass baubles, which Hans Greiner created in current-day Germany in the late 1500s—most Christmas tree decorations were edible, usually apples, pastries, and sweets. Candy canes, one of those sweets, also originated in Germany. Food lore holds that, in 1670, the

From *The Easy Book for Children*, circa 1880

choirmaster of Cologne Cathedral gave white sugar sticks shaped like a shepherd's crosier to the choir children.

Published in 1843, *The Complete Confectioner, Pastry-Cook, and Baker* by James Sanderson includes a recipe for striped peppermint candy sticks. America's National Confectioners Association credits Augustus Imgard—an immigrant from Bavaria to Ohio—with introducing white candy canes to America as a Christmas tree decoration in 1847. The first known occurrence of the term "candy cane" appears in "Tom Luther's Stockings," a short story by M. A. Bates, published in *Ballou's Monthly Magazine* in Boston in 1866.

Twelfth Cake and Christmas Cake

The distant origins of twelfth cakes lie in the ancient Roman festival of Saturnalia. In the Middle Ages, these cakes evolved as merchants and crusaders brought spices from the Silk Road to Europe. In England, the first known mention of cakes for celebrating Twelfth Night occurs around 1570, and the cakes both accompanied the occasion's festivities and contributed to its revels. Confectioners created ever more impressive sugar decorations to top them, and bakers included various tokens or pieces in the batter: a bean for the king (also called the lord of misrule), a pea for the queen, a clove for the knave, a twig for the fool, a piece of rag for the slob, and so on. The recipient of the slice containing the piece played the corresponding role for the rest of the night. Over time, the game evolved into a grand excitement governed by playing cards designating the characters. In France, a similar tradition continues today with *Galette des Rois* (kings' cake), eaten on the 6th of January. The galette is a large pastry filled with almond cream and a tiny figurine (originally a bean). Whoever receives the slice with the figurine becomes king or queen of the day.

But in the 1800s—as the solemn significance of Christmas

eclipsed the raucous revelry of Twelfth Night—the playing tokens devolved into coins, and twelfth cakes waned in popularity. Interestingly, the cookbooks of Acton, Francatelli, and Beeton don't include a recipe for one. Yet as we've seen, the royal household specialised in preserving older culinary traditions. In 1849, John Mawditt, the royal confectioner, made a legendary twelfth cake for Queen Victoria, on which the *Illustrated London News* reported in detail:

> The Cake was of regal dimensions, being about 30 inches in diameter, and tall in proportion: round the side the decorations consisted of strips of gilded paper, bowing outwards near the top, issuing from an elegant gold bordering. The figures, of which there were sixteen, on the top of the Cake, represented a party of beaux and belles of the last century enjoying a repast al fresco, under some trees; whilst others, and some children, were dancing to minstrel strains.
>
> The repast, spread on the ground, with its full complemens of comestibles, decanters, and wine-glasses (the latter, by the way, not sugar glasses, but real brittle ware), was admirably modelled, as were also the figures, servants being represented handing refreshments to some of the gentlemen and ladies, whilst some of the companions of the latter were dancing. The violinist and harpist seemed to be thoroughly impressed with the importance of their functions, and their characteristic attitudes were cleverly given. As a specimen of fancy workmanship, the ornaments to the cake do credit to the skill of Mr. Mawditt.

Queen Victoria's twelfth cake, 1849

After the untimely death of Prince Albert, the prince consort, in 1861, the queen retreated from public life as much as possible and eventually struck Twelfth Night and its decidedly unchristian celebrations from the public calendar. Despite the declining status of the holiday, Charles Dickens continued to cherish the exhilaration of the occasion. His first son, Charles Dickens Jr., was born on the 6th of January 1837. The banking heiress Angela Burdett-Coutts, who was Charley's godmother, famously sent a twelfth cake to the Dickens family every year to celebrate both occasions.

In 1857, the *Englishwoman's Domestic Magazine* ran "Cookery, Pickling, and Preserving," a new column by Isabella Beeton, co-editor of the publication and the wife of its publisher. The column may have seemed like wise words from a veteran housekeeper, but Beeton was just 21 years old, newly married, and had little experience running her own household. Her first cake recipe proved such a disaster that the magazine printed an apology to readers, yet within a few years, Mrs. Beeton had become a household name. She wrote the first known recipe for Christmas cake, which soon supplanted the old tradition of twelfth cake.

"Mrs. Brown had never passed a Christmas in England. The desirability of doing so had often been mooted by her. Her very soul craved the festivities of holly and mince-pies. . . .

Then they all went to church, as a united family ought to do on Christmas-day, and came home to a fine old English early dinner at three o'clock,-a sirloin of beef a foot and a half broad, a turkey as big as an ostrich, a plum-pudding bigger than the turkey, and two or three dozen mince-pies.

'That's a very large bit of beef,' said Mr. Jones, who had not lived much in England latterly.

'It won't look so large,' said the old gentleman, 'when all our friends down-stairs have had their say to it.' 'A plum pudding on Christmas-day can't be too big,' he said again, 'if the cook will but take time enough over it. I never knew a bit to go to waste yet.'"

—From "Christmas at Thompson Hall" by Anthony Trollope, 1876

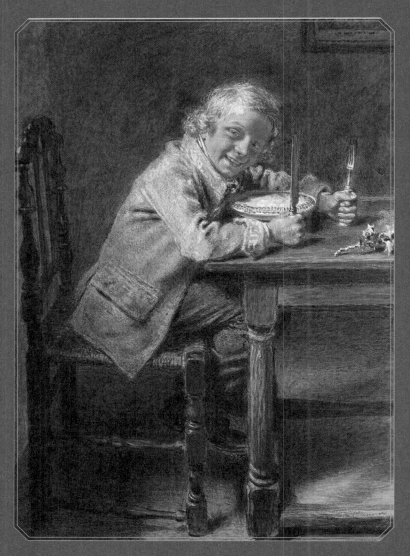

Christmas Pie by William Henry Hunt, 1847

Christmas Recipes

Palestine Soup
ELIZA ACTON

A proper Victorian dinner always began with soup. For Christmas dinner, a house of means would have served this dish, which takes its name from the Jerusalem artichokes that it contains.

1845 RECIPE

Wash and pare quickly some freshly-dug artichokes, and to preserve their colour, throw them into spring-water as they are done, but do not let them remain in it after all are ready. Boil three pounds of them in water for ten minutes; lift them out, and slice them into three pints of boiling stock; when they have stewed gently in this from fifteen to twenty minutes, press them, with the soup, through a fine sieve, and put the whole into a clean saucepan with a pint and a half more of stock; add sufficient salt and cayenne to season it, skim it well, and after it has simmered two or three minutes, stir it into a pint of rich boiling cream. Serve it immediately.

Artichokes, 3 lbs. boiled in water: 10 minutes. Veal stock, 3 pints: 15 to 20 minutes. Additional stock, 1½ pint; little cayenne and salt: 2 to 3 minutes. Boiling cream, 1 pint.

Obs.—The palest veal stock, as for white soup, should be used for this; but for a family dinner, or where economy is a consideration, excellent mutton-broth, made the day before, and perfectly cleared from fat, will answer very well as a substitute; milk, too, may in part take the place of cream, when this last is scarce: the proportion of artichokes should then be increased a little.

Vegetable-marrow, when young, makes a superior soup even to this, which is a most excellent one. It should be well pared, trimmed, and sliced into a small quantity of boiling veal stock, or broth, and when perfectly tender, pressed through a fine sieve, and mixed with more stock, and some cream. In France, the marrow is stewed first in butter, with a large mild onion or two, also sliced; and afterwards in a quart or more of water, which is poured gradually to it; it is next passed through a tammy [strainer], seasoned with pepper and salt, and mixed with a pint or two of milk, and a little cream.

MODERN RECIPE

1½ pounds (680 g) Jerusalem artichokes

1½ pints (850 ml) mushroom stock

⅛ teaspoon cayenne pepper

salt

½ cup (125 ml) heavy / double cream

1. Bring a large pot of water to a boil over medium-high heat. While the water heats, pare the artichokes.

2. Boil the artichokes for 10 minutes. Drain, rinse, and let them cool enough to handle.

3. Slice the boiled artichokes into ½-inch thick pieces.

4. In a medium saucepan over medium-low heat, cook the artichokes in the beef stock for 20 minutes.

5. Transfer the mixture to a blender and purée it until smooth.

6. Return the soup to the saucepan over medium heat. Add the cayenne pepper, salt to taste, and the heavy cream and cook for 2 to 3 more minutes. Strain and serve.

Boiled Turkey with Celery Sauce

CHARLES FRANCATELLI

For Christmas dinner, Victorians usually served turkey either boiled with celery sauce or galantined and stuffed with force-meat (page 26). Cooking turkey by boiling it takes much less time than by roasting. At first glance, the title of this dish may make it seem simple enough, but it still involves a lot of effort. Francatelli cooked for Queen Victoria, after all.

1846 RECIPE

Draw a fine young hen turkey, and remove the angular part of the breast-bone, stuff it with veal stuffing, and truss it for boiling; wrap some buttered paper round it, and place it in an oval braizing-pan with carrot, onion, one head of celery, and a garnished faggot of parsley; add as much white poele [subrecipe], or white stock, as will suffice to cover the turkey, then set it on the stove to boil; it should after that be removed to the side, or placed on a slackened stove to continue gently boiling till done; then take it up out of the braize, remove all the string, &c., and set it to drain upon a napkin; dish it up, pour over it a well-made puree of celery [subrecipe], place round it some stewed heads of celery, and send to table.

Braize for General Purposes.

Take two pounds of fillet of veal, one pound of fat Yorkshire ham, two heads of celery and the same number of onions and carrots; cut all these into small square pieces, add a bayleaf, thyme, parsley, one clove of garlic, two blades of mace, and a dozen cloves; throw these ingredients into a middle sized stewpan in which has been melted down a pound of fresh butter; put the stewpan on the stove-fire, stirring its contents frequently with a wooden spoon while the vegetables, &c. are frying. When this mixture becomes slightly browned, pour into the pan half a pint of Cognac brandy, allow it to simmer for five minutes, and then add three quarts of common broth. Keep the braize gently boiling for an hour and a half, then strain it off through a tammy cloth [cheesecloth] (using considerable pressure) into a kitchen pan, and put it away in the larder.

Purée of Celery.

Cut the white part of six or eight heads of celery into half-inch lengths, boil these in water for five minutes, plunge them in fresh water, and drain the celery in a napkin; then place them in a stewpan with two ounces of butter, some white broth, a little sugar and grated nutmeg; cover the celery thus prepared with a round of buttered paper, place the lid on the stewpan and set it on a slow fire to extract the moisture and melt the celery, taking care that in the course of the process, it does not colour; when the celery is melted or softened, moisten with a ladleful of white sauce, and half a pint of cream; reduce quickly on the fire, stirring the puree the whole time with a wooden spoon. As soon as the puree is reduced to its proper consistency, proceed immediately to rub it through the tammy [strainer], after which take it up into a small stewpan; previously to using it, make the puree hot, and mix with it a little double cream, and a pinch of pounded sugar.

continues ❧

MODERN RECIPE

FOR THE WHITE STOCK

1 pound (450 g) salted butter

2¼ pounds (1 kg)
  protein of choice

1 pound (450 g) ham

2 heads celery

2 carrots

2 medium yellow onions

12 whole cloves

3 or 4 sprigs parsley

1 bay leaf

1 clove garlic

2 blades mace

¼ teaspoon thyme

1 cup (250 ml) brandy

3 quarts (2.8 litres) beef broth

FOR THE TURKEY

1 turkey, 12 to 15 pounds
  (5 to 7 kg), thawed

2¼ pounds (1 kg)
  protein of choice

½ head celery

2 carrots

2 medium yellow onions

10 sprigs parsley

FOR THE CELERY SAUCE

1 head celery

4 tablespoons (½ stick)
  salted butter

1½ cups White Stock

1 tablespoon granulated sugar

1 teaspoon ground nutmeg

1 cup (250 ml) heavy /
  double cream

1. First make the white stock. In a large stockpot or Dutch oven over medium heat, melt the butter.

2. Meanwhile, cut the protein, ham, celery, carrots, and onions into ½-inch cubes and add them to the stockpot.

3. Add the cloves, parsley, bay leaf, garlic, mace, and thyme.

4. Increase the heat to medium-high and cook, stirring frequently, until the mixture browns slightly.

5. Lower the heat to medium-low, add the brandy, and simmer for 5 minutes.

6. Add the beef broth, simmer for 90 minutes, and strain.

7. Meanwhile, prepare the turkey. Stuff it with the protein of choice and truss it for boiling.

8. Place the trussed turkey in a large stockpot or Dutch oven.

9. Cut the celery, onions, and carrots, and onions into ¼-inch chunks and add them to the stockpot, followed by the parsley.

10. Add enough white stock to cover the turkey and, over medium-high heat, bring it to a boil.

11. Reduce the heat to medium-low, cover, and simmer until a leg pulls easily from the bird, 1½ to 2 hours.

12. Meanwhile, make the celery sauce. Chop the celery into ½-inch pieces.

13. In a medium lidded saucepan over medium-high heat, cover the celery with water, bring to a boil, and boil for 5 minutes.

14. Drain and return the boiled celery to the saucepan over medium-low heat.

15. Add the butter, 1 cup (250 ml) of white stock, sugar, and nutmeg. Cover and simmer until the celery softens.

16. Add the remaining ½ cup of white stock and the cream, increase the heat to medium, and stir constantly until the sauce reaches the desired consistency.

17. Transfer to a countertop blender or use an immersion blender and blend until smooth.

18. Transfer the celery sauce to a tureen or saucière and serve.

GALANTINE OF TURKEY
CHARLES FRANCATELLI

An extravagant dish, a galantine consists of poultry or fish that's boned, poached, stuffed, pressed into a cylinder, coated with aspic, and served cold. Forcemeat is a ground mixture of meat, fat, and herbs or spices used for stuffing, such as for sausage. Eliza Acton preferred her forcemeat smooth. In *The Modern Cook*, Francatelli provided a recipe for galantine of poulard (chicken) with aspic jelly and, at the end, added a note that galantine of turkey is made the same way. With the appropriate substitution of turkey for chicken, this recipe demonstrates the enormous complexity and difficulty of daily cooking for wealthy households of the time.

1846 RECIPE

Chop up one pound of white veal, with the same quantity of fat bacon, and season with chopped mushrooms, parsley, nutmeg, pepper, salt, and aromatic seasoning [subrecipe]; when these are chopped quite fine, pound the whole in a mortar, with the yolks of three eggs, and remove the force-meat into a basin. Peel one pound of truffles, and cut up a boiled red tongue, and about one pound of fat bacon or boiled calf's udder, into long narrow fillets, about a quarter of an inch square. Next, bone a fine turkey, and draw the skin from the legs and pinions, inside; then, spread the turkey out upon a napkin, and with a sharp knife, pare off some part of the fillets, to cover the thinner parts of the skin; season lightly with pepper, salt, and aromatic spices; spread a layer of the prepared force-meat, about an inch thick, then place the fillets of tongue and bacon upon this, about an inch apart, and insert

rows of truffles between these: after which, spread another layer
of force-meat over the whole, then repeat the tongue and truffles,
and so on, until a sufficient quantity of both has been placed in
the turkey. It must then be sewn up the back, placed upon a napkin thickly spread with butter, rolled up tightly, and fastened at
each end with string; thus giving to the galantine the appearance
of a cushion. This must be then put into an oval stewpan with
the carcasses and any trimmings of veal or poultry that may be
at hand, also two calf's-feet, two carrots, two onions stuck with
four cloves, a faggot of parsley garnished with green onions, two
bay-leaves, sweet basil and thyme, two blades of mace, and a dozen
pepper-corns; moisten with two glasses of brandy, and set the
pan over a stove-fire to simmer for five minutes, then moisten the
galantine with as much white stock as will suffice to cover it, and
put it back on the stove-fire to boil; it must then be placed upon
a very slow stove-fire, or in the oven, to continue gently braizing
(not boiling), for about two hours and a half. It should then be
removed from the fire, and the galantine taken carefully out of the
napkin; the latter, after being washed in clean hot water, must be
spread out upon the table, and the galantine, after being placed in
it again, and bound up tightly as before, should be put back into

continues ✠

its braize and left in to become partially cold: it must then be put in press between two dishes with a heavy weight upon it. Strain the stock, remove all the grease from the surface, and clarify it in the usual manner, then pass it through a napkin or a jelly-bag, and place it on some rough ice to become firmly set. When the galantine is quite cold, take it out of the napkin, and use a clean cloth to absorb any moisture or grease there may be on the surface; it must then be glazed, and placed upon its dish. Decorate it with aspic jelly . . . and serve.

Aromatic-Spices, for Seasoning.

Take of nutmegs, and mace, one ounce each; of cloves, and white pepper-corns, two ounces each; of sweet-basil, marjoram, and thyme, one ounce each, and half an ounce of bay-leaves: these herbs should be previously dried for the purpose: roughly pound the spices, then place the whole of the above ingredients between two sheets of strong white paper, and after the sides have been twisted or folded over tightly, so as to prevent as much as possible the evaporation of the volatile properties of the herbs and spices, place them on a baking-sheet in the skreen to become perfectly dry; they must then be pounded quickly, sifted through a fine hair-sieve, corked up tightly in a dry bottle, and kept for use.

Roast Goose with Sage and Onion Stuffing

ISABELLA BEETON

Only 15 years separate Francatelli's *Modern Cook* from *Mrs. Beeton's Book of Household Management*, but they stand worlds apart from each other. Beeton's text follows Eliza Acton's cookbook conventions: ingredient lists, detailed measures, cooking times, and paragraphs, all conventions that recipes still use today. In a time with a looser appreciation for intellectual property rights, Beeton copied many of Acton's recipes and adapted others, including this one.

continues 𝕂-

1861 RECIPE

INGREDIENTS.—Goose, 4 large onions, 10 sage-leaves, ¼ lb. of bread crumbs, 1½ oz. of butter, salt and pepper to taste, 1 egg.

Choosing and Trussing.—Select a goose with a clean white skin, plump breast, and yellow feet: if these latter are red, the bird is old. Should the weather permit, let it hang for a few days: by so doing, the flavour will be very much improved. Pluck, singe, draw, and carefully wash and wipe the goose; cut off the neck close to the back, leaving the skin long enough to turn over; cut off the feet at the first joint, and separate the pinions at the first joint. Beat the breast-bone flat with a rolling-pin, put a skewer through the under part of each wing, and having drawn up the legs closely, put a skewer into the middle of each, and pass the same quite through the body. Insert another skewer into the small of the leg, bring it close down to the side bone, run it through, and do the same to the other side. Now cut off the end of the Vent, and make a hole in the skin sufficiently large for the passage of the rump, in order to keep in the seasoning.

Mode.—Make a sage-and-onion stuffing of the above ingredients [subrecipe]; put it into the body of the goose, and secure it firmly at both ends, by passing the rump through the hole made in the skin, and the other end by tying the skin of the neck to the back; by this means the seasoning will not escape. Put it down to a brisk fire, keep it well basted, and roast from 1½ to 2 hours, according to the size. Remove the skewers, and serve with a tureen of good gravy, and one of well-made apple-sauce. Should a very highly-flavoured seasoning be preferred, the onions should not be parboiled, but minced raw: of the two methods, the mild seasoning is far superior. A ragoût, or pie, should be made of the giblets, or they may be stewed down to make gravy. Be careful to serve the goose before the breast falls, or its appearance will be spoiled by coming flattened to table. As this is rather a troublesome joint to carve, a large quantity of gravy should not be poured round the goose, but sent in a tureen.

Time.—A large goose, 1¾ hour; a moderate-sized one, 1¼ to 1½ hour.

Seasonable from September to March; but in perfection from Michaelmas to Christmas.

Average cost, 5s. 6d. each.

Sufficient for 8 or 9 persons.

Note.—A teaspoonful of made mustard, a saltspoonful of salt, a few grains of cayenne, mixed with a glass of port wine, are sometimes poured into the goose by a slit made in the apron. This sauce is, by many persons, considered an improvement.

Sage-and-Onion Stuffing, for Geese, Ducks, and Pork.

INGREDIENTS.—4 large onions, 10 sage-leaves, ¼ lb. of bread crumbs, 1½ oz. of butter, salt and pepper to taste, 1 egg.

Mode.—Peel the onions, put them into boiling water, let them simmer for 5 minutes or rather longer, and, just before they are taken out, put in the sage-leaves for a minute or two to take off their rawness. Chop both these very fine, add the bread, seasoning, and butter, and work the whole together with the yolk of an egg,

continues ❦

when the stuffing will be ready for use. It should be rather highly seasoned, and the sage-leaves should be very finely chopped. Many cooks do not parboil the onions in the manner just stated, but merely use them raw. The stuffing then, however, is not nearly so mild, and, to many tastes, its strong flavour would be very objectionable. When made for goose, a portion of the liver of the bird, simmered for a few minutes and very finely minced, is frequently added to this stuffing; and where economy is studied, the egg may be dispensed with.

Time.—Rather more than 5 minutes to simmer the onions.

Average cost, for this quantity, 4d.

Sufficient for 1 goose, or a pair of ducks.

CHESTNUT STUFFING
CEDRIC DICKENS

A great-grandson of Charles and Catherine Dickens, Cedric Dickens wrote several books, including *Dining with Dickens* and *Drinking with Dickens*, which used and adapted many family recipes from the 1800s, including this one.

2 stalks celery

1 large white onion

2 tablespoons (¼ stick) unsalted butter

3½ ounces (100 g) mushrooms

15 ounces (425 g) unsweetened chestnut purée

4 ounces (113 g) breadcrumbs

1 large egg

1 tablespoon brandy

salt and pepper

1. Thinly slice the celery and chop the onion.

2. In a medium saucepan over medium-high heat, add the butter and sauté the celery and onion until soft and translucent, 5 minutes.

3. Add the mushrooms and sauté for 3 to 4 minutes.

4. Remove from the heat and add the chestnut purée and breadcrumbs.

5. Let cool for 1 to 2 minutes.

6. Stir in the egg and brandy, add salt and pepper to taste, and serve.

BRUSSELS SPROUTS ON BUTTERED TOAST
ELIZA ACTON

Acton's recipe, easy enough to follow in the original, helpfully touches on how other countries, namely Belgium and France, prepared this traditional Christmas vegetable.

1845 RECIPE

These delicate little sprouts, or miniature cabbages, should be gathered when not larger than a common walnut, and after being trimmed free from any decayed leaves, and washed very thoroughly, should be thrown into a pan of water properly salted, and boiled from eight to ten minutes, then well drained, and served upon a rather thick round of toasted bread, buttered on both sides. Rich melted butter must be sent to table with them. This is the Belgian mode of dressing this excellent vegetable, which is served in France with the sauce poured over it, or it is tossed in a stewpan with a slice of butter and some pepper and salt: a spoonful or two of veal gravy (and sometimes a little lemon-juice) is added when these are perfectly mixed.

8 to 10 minutes.

BOILED ASPARAGUS ON TOAST

ISABELLA BEETON

Many wealthy households served asparagus for Christmas dinner. This recipe echoes parts of Francatelli's recipe for Asparagus with White Sauce, but Beeton simplifies it, replacing the white butter sauce with melted butter.

1861 RECIPE

INGREDIENTS.—To each ½ gallon of water allow 1 heaped tablespoonful of salt; asparagus.

Mode.—Asparagus should be dressed as soon as possible after it is cut, although it may be kept for a day or two by putting the stalks into cold water; yet, to be good, like every other vegetable, it cannot be cooked too fresh. Scrape the white part of the stems, *beginning* from the head, and throw them into cold water; then tie them into bundles of about 20 each, keeping the heads all one way, and cut the stalks evenly, that they may all be the same length; put them into boiling water, with salt in the above proportion; keep them boiling quickly until tender, with the saucepan uncovered. When the asparagus is done, dish it upon toast, which should be dipped in the water it was cooked in, and leave the white ends outwards each way, with the points meeting in the middle. Serve with a tureen of melted butter.

Time.—15 to 18 minutes after the water boils.

Average cost, in full season, 2s. 6d. the 100 heads.

Sufficient.—Allow about 50 heads for 4 or 5 persons.

Seasonable.—May be had, forced, from January but cheapest in May, June, and July.

MINCEMEAT PIE
ELIZA ACTON

Golden Pippin apples are gold with russet dotting on the skin. They have a bracing taste with a lemony tang. If you can't find them, use a mix of other mildly tart heirloom apples, such as Cortland, Empire, Granny Smith, Jonathan, Liberty, or Winesap. After you've made your mincemeat, refrigerate it, covered, for at least 8 hours but ideally 24 for the flavours to incorporate. Acton's recipe for pie crust follows, which you can modify with lard or vegetable shortening in place of suet. When ready to bake, preheat the oven to 400°F (205°C; gas mark 6). Add bottom crusts to 9-inch glass pie plates, fill with mincemeat, and top with second crusts. Flute the edges and slit the tops in several places. Bake on the lowest rack until the pastry turns golden brown, 40 to 45 minutes. Let cool to room temperature before serving.

1845 RECIPE

Superlative Mincemeat.

Take four large lemons, with their weight of golden pippins pared and cored, of jar-raisins, currants, candied citron and orange-rind, and the finest suet, and a fourth part more of pounded sugar. Boil the lemons tender, chop them small, but be careful first to extract all the pips; add them to the other ingredients, after all have been prepared with great nicety, and mix the whole *well* with from three to four glasses of good brandy. Apportion salt and spice by the preceding receipt [salt, ½ oz.; nutmegs, 2 small; pounded mace, 1 large teaspoonful, and rather more of ginger]. We think that the weight of one lemon, in meat, improves this mixture; or, in lieu of it, a small quantity of crushed macaroons added just before it is baked.

Common Suet-Crust for Pies.

In many families this is preferred both for pies and tarts, to crust made with butter, as being much more wholesome; but it should never be served unless especially ordered, as it is to some persons peculiarly distasteful. Chop the suet extremely small, and add from six to eight ounces of it to a pound of flour, with a few grains of salt; mix these with cold water into a firm paste, and work it very smooth. Some cooks beat it with a paste-roller, until the suet is perfectly blended with flour; but the crust is lighter without this. In exceedingly sultry weather the suet, not being firm enough to chop, may be sliced as thin as possible, and well beaten into the paste after it is worked up.

Flour, 2 lbs.; beef or veal kidney-suet, 12 to 16 oz.; salt (for fruit-pies), ¼ teaspoonful.

Mince Pies

CHRISTMAS PUDDING
ELIZA ACTON

The first edition of *Modern Cookery for Private Families* contains three different recipes for Christmas pudding: Ingoldsby Christmas Puddings, Cottage Christmas Pudding, and The Author's Christmas Pudding, the last of which appears below. Both Queen Victoria and her husband, Prince Albert, were German, so two of Acton's recipes for German pudding sauce follow.

1845 RECIPE

To three ounces of flour, and the same weight of fine, lightly grated bread-crumbs, add six of beef kidney-suet, chopped small, six of raisins weighed after they are stoned, six of well-cleaned currants, four ounces of minced apples, five of sugar, two of candied orange rind, half a teaspoonful of nutmeg mixed with pounded mace, a very little salt, a small glass of brandy, and three whole eggs. Mix and beat these ingredients well together, tie them tightly in a thickly floured cloth, and boil them for three hours and a half. We can recommend this as a remarkably light small rich pudding; it may be served with German, wine, or punch sauce.

Flour, 3 ozs.; bread-crumbs, 3 ozs.; suet, stoned raisins, and currants, each, 6 ozs.; minced apples, 4 ozs.; sugar, 5 ozs.; candied peel, 2 ozs.; spice, ½ teaspoonful; salt, few grains; brandy, small wineglassful; eggs, 3: 3½ hours.

A Delicious German Pudding Sauce.

Dissolve in half a pint of sherry or of Madeira, from three to four ounces of fine sugar, but do not allow the wine to boil; stir it hot to the well-beaten yolks of six fresh eggs, and mill the sauce over a gentle fire until it is well thickened, and highly frothed; pour it over a plum, or any other kind of sweet boiled pudding, of which it much improves the appearance. Half the quantity will be sufficient for one of moderate size. A small machine, resembling a chocolate mill, is used in Germany for frothing this sauce; but a couple of silver forks, fastened together at the handles, will serve for the purpose, on an emergency. We recommend the addition of a dessertspoonful of strained lemon-juice to the wine.

For large pudding, sherry or Madeira, ½ pint; fine sugar, 3 to 4 ozs.; yolks of eggs, 6; lemon-juice (if added), 1 dessertspoonful.

Obs.—The safer plan with sauces liable to curdle is to thicken them always in a jar or jug, placed in a saucepan of water; when this is not done, they should be held over the fire, but never placed *upon* it.

A German Custard Pudding-Sauce.

Boil very gently together half a pint of new milk or of milk and cream mixed, a very thin strip or two of fresh lemon-rind, a bit of cinnamon, half an inch of a vanilla bean, and an ounce and a half or two ounces of sugar, until the milk is strongly flavoured; then strain, and pour it, by slow degrees, to the well-beaten yolks of three eggs, smoothly mixed with a knife-end-full (about half a teaspoonful) of flour, a grain or two of salt, and a tablespoonful of cold milk; and stir these very quickly round as the milk is added. Put the sauce again into the stewpan, and whisk or stir it rapidly until it thickens, and looks creamy. It must not be placed upon the fire, but should be held over it, when this is done.

continues

The Germans mill their sauces to a froth; but they may be whisked with almost equally good effect, though a small mill for the purpose—formed like a chocolate mill—may be had at a very trifling cost.

MODERN RECIPE

FOR THE PUDDING

1 apple, approximately
 3¾ ounces (110 g)

3 ounces (85 g)
 all-purpose flour

3 ounces (85 g)
 white breadcrumbs

6 ounces (170 g)
 vegetable shortening

6 ounces (170 g) raisins

6 ounces (170 g) currants or
 sultanas / golden raisins

5 ounces (140 g) dark
 brown sugar

2 ounces (55 g) diced candied
 orange peel

½ teaspoon ground nutmeg

½ teaspoon mace

1 pinch salt

½ cup (125 ml) brandy

3 eggs

unsalted butter for greasing

FOR THE GERMAN PUDDING SAUCE

½ cup (125 ml) Sherry
 or Madeira

2 ounces (55 g)
 granulated sugar

3 egg yolks

½ teaspoon lemon juice

1. Peel, core, and mince the apple.

2. In a large mixing bowl, combine the flour, breadcrumbs, shortening, raisins, currants or sultanas, apples, sugar, orange peel, nutmeg, mace, and salt.

3. In a small bowl, whisk together the brandy and eggs. Add the egg brandy to the dry ingredients and stir to combine thoroughly.

4. Grease a 2-pint (1.25 litre) pudding mould with butter.

5. Firmly press the raw pudding all the way into the mould, leaving about ¼ inch (5 mm) of space at the top.

6. Cut parchment paper to fit the mould and place it on the pudding. Cover the mould with foil tented in the middle.

7. With kitchen string, fashion a handle for the mould so you can lower it into and lift it from the boiling water safely.

8. Fill a large lidded pot with enough water so that, with the mould in it, the water rises between ⅔ of the way up the side of the mould and 1 inch (2.5 cm) from the top.

9. In the bottom of the pot, place a small plate, upside down, to prevent what will become the top of the pudding from scorching.

10. Place the pot over medium-high heat and gently lower the mould into the water onto the underside of the plate.

11. When the water boils, reduce the heat to medium-low and simmer for 3 to 4 hours, depending on the size of the mould, until the pudding darkens. Add water as necessary to maintain the level.

12. If making on Christmas, invert the mould onto a serving platter to plate the pudding and proceed to step 16.

13. If making on Stir-Up Sunday, store the cooked pudding in the mould in a cool, dark place. When ready to serve, replace the tented foil lid and simmer again for 1 hour.

14. Before serving, make the pudding sauce. In a small saucepan over medium-low heat, add the Sherry or Madeira and the sugar and stir until the sugar dissolves. Don't let the mixture boil.

15. Meanwhile, in a small bowl, beat the egg yolks with the lemon juice.

16. Add the beaten yolks to a double boiler or similar. Add the fortified wine mixture to the yolks and whisk continuously until the mixture thickens and becomes foamy.

17. Pour the sauce over the warm pudding and serve.

"Once a Year" from a picture by W. Kumpel, from the *Illustrated London News*

PLUM PUDDING
CHARLES FRANCATELLI

A year after the publication of Eliza Acton's cookbook, Francatelli's followed. In it, he mentions Christmas only twice—when touching on the seasonal demand for Yorkshire pies and for a dish called Hunting Beef—but he still provides a suitably German recipe for plum pudding for celebrating the holiday. A gill is a quarter of a pint, or 142 ml, and from an older usage, "plum" means what we call raisins, not the larger stone fruit as we know it today.

1846 RECIPE

Ingredients:—Three quarters of a pound of raisins, three quarters of a pound of currants, half a pound of candied orange, lemon, and citron, one pound and a quarter of chopped beef suet, one pound of flour, three quarters of a pound of moist sugar, four eggs, about, three gills of milk, the grated rind of two lemons, half an ounce of nutmeg, cinnamon and cloves (in powder), a glass of brandy and a very little salt.

Mix the above ingredients thoroughly together in a large basin several hours before the pudding is to be boiled; pour them into a mould spread with butter, which should be tied up in a cloth. The pudding must then be boiled for four hours and a half; when done, dish it up with a German custard sauce spread over it.

continues

German-Custard-Sauce

Put four yolks of eggs into a bain-marie or stewpan, together with two ounces of pounded sugar, a glass of Sherry, some orange or lemon peel (rubbed on loaf sugar), and a very little salt. Whisk this sharply over a very slow fire, until it assumes the appearance of a light frothy custard.

MODERN RECIPE

FOR THE PUDDING

12 ounces (340 g) raisins

12 ounces (340 g) currants

2⅔ ounces (75 g) candied citron peel

2⅔ ounces (75 g) candied lemon peel

2⅔ ounces (75 g) candied orange peel

1¼ pounds (567 g) chopped beef or vegetable suet

1 pound (455 g) all-purpose flour

12 ounces (340 g) granulated sugar

4 medium eggs

¾ pint (425 ml) whole / full-fat milk

grated zest of 2 lemons

1 teaspoon ground cinnamon

1 teaspoon ground nutmeg

½ teaspoon ground cloves

¼ cup (60 ml) brandy

1 pinch salt

unsalted butter for greasing

FOR THE GERMAN CUSTARD SAUCE

¼ cup (60 ml) Sherry

2 ounces (55 g) powdered sugar

4 egg yolks

½ ounce (15 g) diced candied orange or lemon peel

1 pinch salt

1. In a large mixing bowl, thoroughly combine all the pudding ingredients.

2. Grease a large pudding mould with butter.

3. Follow the Christmas Pudding method (page 40), steps 5 through 10.

4. When the water boils, reduce the heat to medium-low and simmer the pudding for 4½ hours. Add water as necessary to maintain the level.

5. While the pudding is boiling, make the pudding sauce. In a small saucepan over medium-low heat, add the Sherry and sugar and stir until the sugar dissolves. Don't let the mixture boil.

6. Meanwhile, in a small bowl, beat the egg yolks.

7. Add the beaten yolks to a double boiler or similar. Add the fortified wine mixture, candied citrus peel, and salt to the yolks and whisk continuously until the mixture thickens and becomes foamy.

8. When the pudding is done boiling, invert the mould onto a serving platter to plate it.

9. Pour the sauce over the warm pudding and serve.

VEGETARIAN PLUM PUDDING

FRANCES BOULT

Victorian vegetarians didn't eat traditional plum pudding, Christmas or otherwise, because it contains beef suet. A member of the British Women's Temperance Association, Frances Boult initially went vegetarian to help treat paralysis, but she later embraced the ethics of the movement. She founded the Northern Heights Vegetarian Society, the Ivy Leaf Society for vegetarian children, and *Children's Garden* magazine. In the late 1890s, she created this short, simple recipe, which the Order of the Golden Age, an animal rights society, published. You can use vegetable shortening in place of suet in Eliza Acton's Christmas Pudding (page 38) or use these ingredients with that method. To make it vegan, replace the dairy milk with coconut or soy milk and the eggs with 4 tablespoons of ground flaxseed in 12 tablespoons of water or 4 tablespoons of chia seeds in 10 tablespoons of water.

1890S RECIPE

Use four ounces of tapioca soaked in one pint of cold water for twelve hours, one pound and a half of wholemeal bread crumbs, eight ounces of sugar, four pounds stoned raisins, one pound carrots grated and mashed very fine, four eggs, half a pint of milk.

TWELFTH CAKE
JOHN MOLLARD

The earliest known recipe for twelfth cake comes from *The Art of Cookery: Made Easy and Refined* by John Mollard, published in 1802 at the apex of the cake's public popularity.

1802 RECIPE

Take seven pounds of flour, make a cavity in the centre, set a sponge with a gill and a half of yeast and a little warm milk; then put round it one pound of fresh butter broke into small lumps, one pound and a quarter of sifted sugar, four pounds and a half of currants washed and picked, half an ounce of sifted cinnamon, a quarter of an ounce of pounded cloves, mace, and nutmeg mixed, sliced candied orange or lemon peel and citron. When the sponge is risen, mix all the ingredients together with a little warm milk; let the hoops be well papered and buttered, then fill them with the mixture and bake them, and when nearly cold ice them over with sugar prepared for that purpose as per receipt; or they may be plain.

CHRISTMAS CAKE
ISABELLA BEETON

Since her death at age 28, Beeton's reputation has taken a beating as researchers discovered the extent to which she copied or took credit for recipes by or from others. She does receive credit, however, for penning the first recipe for Christmas cake. As a unit of measure, a teacup is a scant ¾ cup.

1861 RECIPE

INGREDIENTS.—5 teacupfuls of flour, 1 teacupful of melted butter, 1 teacupful of cream, 1 teacupful of treacle, 1 teacupful of moist sugar, 2 eggs, ½ oz. of powdered ginger, ½ lb. of raisins, 1 teaspoonful of carbonate of soda, 1 tablespoonful of vinegar.

Mode.—Make the butter sufficiently warm to melt it, but do not allow it to oil; put the flour into a basin; add to it the sugar, ginger, and raisins, which should be stoned and cut into small pieces. When these dry ingredients are thoroughly mixed, stir in the butter, cream, treacle, and well-whisked eggs, and beat the mixture for a few minutes. Dissolve the soda in the vinegar, add it to the dough, and be particular that these latter ingredients are well incorporated with the others; put the cake into a buttered mould or tin, place it in a moderate oven immediately, and bake it from 1¾ to 2¼ hours.

Time.—1¾ to 2¼ hours.

Average cost, 1s. 6d.

CHOCOLATE YULE LOG

PIERRE LACAM

In France, burning a Yule log remained a popular holiday activity until the rise of Napoléon Bonaparte. Bonaparte banned the practice reportedly from a concern that burning such a large log at home would make people ill. The tradition continued, however, in the form of making and eating this *bûche de Noël*. The first known recipe appears in *Le Mémorial Historique et Géographique de la Pâtisserie*, a masterwork of 1,600 recipes by Pierre Lacam, who had served as pâtissier to Prince Charles III of Monaco in the late 1870s. Lacam's *bûche de Noël* consists of a genoise (sponge roll cake) filled and covered with mocha buttercream textured to simulate tree bark.

1890 RECIPE

Bûche de Noël

Elle se fait en biscuit à la poche, et en génoise sur plaque. En biscuit, c'est plus coûteux pour la crème, vu les cintre des bouchées. La génoise est chère par sa pâte et ses rognures, mais n'a pas de cintres à boucher. Prenon la génoise, vous coupez une dizaine de ronds égaux, je suppose, vous les collez l'un contre l'autre à la crème moka ou chocolat. Vous masquez bien tout autour et lissez. Vous la couchez sur un fond allongé parsemé d'amandes grillées. Vous la décorez d'un bout à l'autre à la fine douille à breton, bien égale, imitant l'écorce de l'arbre, et après, vous y posez quatre ou cinq noeuds en biscuit épais coupés à l'emporte-pièce imitant les noeuds de branches, vous les masquez et les décorez de bas en haut même douille, l'on masque les deux extrémités de la bûche sans décorer.

continues ❧

Il y a des maisons qui passent avec pression de la pâte d'amandes verte à la passoire, d'autres sèment des pistaches hachées très fines. On en fait à la meringue italienne, mais ferme.

[translation]

It's made like a small sponge cake, known as a genoise, on a baking sheet. The sponge cake uses much more cream because of the size of the bites. The sponge cake requires more dough for its trimmings and to create knots poking from the cake. Cut about ten equal discs of the sponge cake and affix them, one against the other, with the mocha or chocolate cream. Frost it well, all around and smooth. Place it on an elongated platter sprinkled with toasted almonds. Decorate it from one end to the other with a fine Breton nozzle, very evenly, imitating the bark of the tree. Place four or five thick biscuit knots cut with a cookie cutter to imitate the knots of branches. Cover them and decorate them from bottom to top, in one movement. Frost the two ends of the log without decorating. Some houses pass raw almond paste through a strainer to decorate. Others use pistachios chopped very finely. We make it with a firm Italian meringue.

MODERN RECIPE

FOR THE CHOCOLATE GENOISE

7 large eggs, at
   room temperature

10 egg yolks, at
   room temperature

1 teaspoon salt

9 ounces (255 g)
   granulated sugar

7 ounces (200 g) cake flour

2 ounces (55 g) Dutch process
   cocoa powder

1 teaspoon vanilla extract

2 tablespoons (28 g)
   unsalted butter

FOR THE MOCHA BUTTERCREAM

3 cups (335 g) powdered /
  icing sugar

1½ cups (340 g) unsalted butter,
  at room temperature

1 ounce (30 ml) hot water

2 tablespoons dark roast
  instant coffee

2 teaspoons vanilla extract

4 tablespoons Dutch process
  cocoa powder

1. Preheat the oven to 350°F (180°C; gas mark 4).

2. In the bowl of a stand mixer fitted with the whisk attachment, beat the eggs, yolks, and salt on medium speed until thoroughly combined.

3. Increase the speed to high, gradually add the sugar, and beat for 10 minutes.

4. Meanwhile, in a medium bowl, sift the flour and cocoa powder three times.

5. Add the vanilla to the egg mixture and beat to incorporate fully.

6. In the microwave, heat the butter on high in intervals of 15 or 20 seconds until melted.

7. With a pastry brush, butter a rimmed baking sheet.

8. Cut a piece of parchment paper to fit the baking sheet, place it on the buttered sheet, and butter the paper.

9. With a soft spatula, fold a third of the cocoa flour into the egg mixture and stir gently to incorporate.

10. Repeat twice more with the remaining cocoa flour.

11. Pour the batter into the prepared baking dish and spread it into an even layer.

12. Bake until the top is dry and springs back when lightly pressed, 20 to 25 minutes. Remove it from the oven and let it cool for 10 minutes.

continues

13. Meanwhile, make the mocha buttercream. In the bowl of a stand mixer fitted with the flat beater attachment, sift the powdered sugar.

14. Add the butter and cream it on medium speed until light and fluffy, about 2 minutes.

15. In a small glass, add the hot water and dissolve the instant coffee in it.

16. Add the coffee and the vanilla extract to the mixer and beat, occasionally scraping down the sides, to incorporate fully.

17. Transfer half the buttercream to another bowl for filling the genoise.

18. Add the cocoa powder to the buttercream still in the stand mixer bowl and beat to combine fully. Cover the mocha buttercream and refrigerate until ready to frost the log.

19. When the cake has cooled, use an offset spatula to spread the plain buttercream into an even layer on the cake. Leave a ½-inch border on the outside edges of the genoise to allow the buttercream to expand and move when rolling.

20. Using the parchment paper for help, slowly roll the cake from one of the long ends into a log. Carefully remove the paper as you roll.

21. To make small stumps or branches for the finished log, cut small slices from the end(s) of the roll. For stumps, leave the slices as they are. For branches, unroll and trim as needed. Refrigerate until ready to use.

22. Plate the roll on a serving platter, seam side down, and refrigerate until cold, 30 minutes to 1 hour.

23. Spread the mocha buttercream over the entire roll, reserving some if affixing any stumps or branches.

24. Place or attach the stumps or branches and frost them in place with mocha buttercream so no seams show.

25. With a cake comb or fork, rake the mocha buttercream to resemble tree bark. Slice diagonally to serve.

CRATCHIT CHRISTMAS TWIST

In *A Christmas Carol*, Bob Cratchit makes a version of a gin twist, a popular Victorian drink, for his family: "Bob, turning up his cuffs—as if, poor fellow, they were capable of being made more shabby—compounded some hot mixture in a jug with gin and lemons, and stirred it round and round and put it on the hob to simmer."

1 cup (250 ml) water
1 cup (200 g) granulated sugar
2 lemons

1 cup (250 ml) Old Tom
or Plymouth gin

1. First make the simple syrup. In a kettle, saucepan, or microwave, heat the water until almost boiling.

2. Add the sugar and stir to dissolve it completely. Let cool to room temperature and then refrigerate, covered or sealed, until ready to use.

3. Use a Y-shaped vegetable peeler to peel from each lemon 2 strips of peel about 3 inches long and ½ inch wide, taking care not to remove any pith. Set the 4 peels aside.

4. Juice the lemons for 4 ounces (125 ml) of juice.

5. Boil a kettle of water and chafe 4 Irish coffee mugs.

6. Into each prepared mug, pour 2 ounces (60 ml) of gin, 2 ounces (60 ml) of simple syrup, and 1 ounce (30 ml) of lemon juice. Top with hot water to taste.

7. Rub the outside edge of a lemon peel around the mouth of each mug. Place the peel, skin side down, over the drink and twist it to express the citrus oils, then add to the glass as garnish.

8. Serve hot and sip slowly.

Smoking Bishop Punch

CEDRIC DICKENS

At the end of *A Christmas Carol*, Ebenezer Scrooge invites Bob Cratchit to share this drink with him: "I'll raise your salary, and endeavour to assist your struggling family, and we will discuss your affairs this very afternoon, over a Christmas bowl of smoking bishop, Bob!" This popular nineteenth-century drink showcased expensive, imported ingredients: oranges from Spain, wine from France and Portugal, and sugar from current-day Guyana. Only the wealthy could afford to drink it. Along with most punches, it has faded from popular consumption, but the Charles Dickens Museum in London serves it at Christmas events. It packs a punch, so pour it lightly and enjoy it slowly!

6 Seville oranges

30 whole cloves

½ cup (100 g) Demerara sugar

1 bottle red wine (Cabernet Sauvignon, Grenache, Malbec, Merlot, or Syrah)

1 bottle ruby Port

1 stick cinnamon

1. Preheat the oven to 325°F (205°C; gas mark 6).

2. Wash and dry the oranges.

3. Stud each of the oranges with 5 cloves.

4. On an unlined baking sheet, roast the studded oranges for 1 hour.

5. Place the roasted oranges in a large punch bowl.

6. Add the sugar and the bottle of red wine.

7. Cover the bowl and let the oranges macerate in a cool place or refrigerator for 12 to 24 hours.

8. Remove the cloves from the oranges and use a Y-shaped vegetable peeler to peel strips of orange peel for garnish. Set peels aside.

Scrooge and Cratchit drinking Smoking Bishop Punch

9. Halve the oranges and juice them through a strainer into the wine mixture.

10. Transfer the mixture to a large saucepan over medium-low heat.

11. Add the bottle of Port and the cinnamon stick and heat the mixture, but don't let it boil.

12. Ladle it into teacups, Irish coffee mugs, or other heatproof glasses, garnishing each with a strip of reserved orange peel.

EGGNOG

ELIZA ACTON

From the 1300s, we have this holiday favourite, though, as with many ancient dishes, it likely dates back further than that. *The Oxford English Dictionary* defines "nog" as a strong ale brewed in East Anglia, with the first record of it dating to 1693. It also could come from the Irish word *naigín*, meaning a small wooden cup. George Washington served the drink in Virginia, and the compound word "eggnog" comes from America, around 1775. A similar drink, milk punch, also enters the scene in the late 1600s (first mention) and early 1700s (first recipe). Milk punch doesn't require eggs, though Acton added them, as recorded in this recipe from the 1859 edition of her cookbook. In the Victorian era, only the wealthy would have drunk eggnog because of the considerable expense of its ingredients.

1859 RECIPE

Cambridge Milk Punch.

Throw into two quarts of new milk the very thinly-pared rind of a fine lemon, and half a pound of good sugar in lumps; bring it slowly to boil, take out the lemon-rind, draw it from the fire, and stir quickly in a couple of well-whisked eggs which have been mixed with less than half a pint of cold milk, and strained th[r]ough a sieve; the milk must not of course be allowed to boil after these are mixed with it. Add gradually a pint of rum, and half a pint of brandy; mill the punch to a froth, and serve it immediately with quite warm glasses. At the University the lemon-rind is usually omitted, but it is a great improvement to the flavour of the beverage. The sugar and spirit can be otherwise apportioned to the taste; and we would recommend the yolks of three eggs, or of four, in preference to the two whole ones.

New milk, 2 quarts; rind, 1 large lemon; fresh eggs, 2; cold milk, ½ pint; rum, 1 pint; brandy, ½ pint.

MODERN RECIPE

2½ cups (600 ml) whole / full-fat milk

3⅓ ounces (100 ml) heavy / double cream

1 teaspoon vanilla extract

2 sticks cinnamon

3 cloves

1 teaspoon freshly grated nutmeg, plus more for garnish

3 large eggs

½ cup (100 g) golden superfine / caster sugar

3⅓ ounces (100 ml) brandy or rum (optional)

ground cinnamon for garnish

continues ✺

1. In a small saucepan over medium-low heat, add the milk, cream, vanilla, cinnamon sticks, cloves, and nutmeg. Stir occasionally until the mixture is just about to boil. Remove from the heat and let cool to room temperature.

2. Separate the eggs. In an airtight container, refrigerate the whites until ready to serve.

3. In a medium bowl, whisk together the egg yolks and sugar until well combined.

4. When the cream mixture has cooled, remove the cloves and cinnamon sticks.

5. Pour the cream mixture into the egg yolks and sugar and whisk to eliminate any lumps.

6. Return the eggnog to the saucepan over low heat and stir continuously until slightly thickened. Whisk again to eliminate any lumps.

7. Remove from the heat and let cool to room temperature. If adding alcohol, do so now.

8. Refrigerate for at least 1 hour but preferably overnight.

9. When ready to serve, beat the egg whites in a stand mixer fitted with a whisk attachment or with an immersion blender until they form soft peaks.

10. Carefully fold the egg whites into the chilled eggnog, stir gently to combine, and pour into cups or glasses.

11. Garnish with a little more grated nutmeg and ground cinnamon.

VEGAN NOG

Vegan drinks may not sound very Victorian, but almond milk beverages—usually served warm and sweetened—have existed for centuries and appear in Victorian cookbooks. Chefs and cooks of the time also used coconuts to create sauces and desserts, with coconut cake and coconut ice proving particularly popular. To create a good vegan eggnog, you need to achieve thickness and creaminess without using eggs. The secret lies in the cornstarch/corn flour!

2 teaspoons warm water

1 teaspoon cornstarch/
corn flour

2½ cups (600 ml) almond milk

1 cup (200 g) coconut cream

4 tablespoons (50 g)
granulated sugar

1 teaspoon vanilla extract

2 sticks cinnamon, plus more
for garnish

3 whole cloves

1 teaspoon freshly grated
nutmeg, plus more
for garnish

3⅓ ounces (100 ml) brandy
or rum (optional)

1. In a small glass, add the warm water and stir in the cornstarch/ corn flour to form a paste.

2. In a small saucepan over medium-low heat, add the almond milk, coconut cream, cornstarch/corn flour paste, and sugar. Stir to eliminate any lumps.

3. Add the vanilla extract, cinnamon sticks, cloves, and nutmeg and stir for 2 or 3 minutes. Don't let the mixture boil.

4. Remove from the heat and let cool. If serving warm, add the alcohol, if using, and proceed to step 6. If serving cold, let cool to room temperature, then add the alcohol, if using.

continues 〰️

5. Refrigerate for at least 1 hour but preferably overnight.

6. When ready to serve, remove the cloves and cooked cinnamon sticks.

7. Pour the nog into glasses or cups, grate some fresh nutmeg over each, add a fresh cinnamon stick, and serve.

HOT SPICED APPLE JUICE

Apples grew widely in Victorian Britain, making them available and affordable to most people. Britain never had a period of prohibition—with even the Puritans drinking alcohol—but the temperance movement grew in the 1800s. Many temperance followers and supporters who abstained from alcohol quaffed a version of this seasonal drink.

8½ cups (2 litres) fresh apple juice

2 tablespoons honey

1 teaspoon freshly grated ginger

strips of peel from 2 oranges and 4 limes

2 sticks cinnamon

10 cloves

1 apple for garnish

1. In a large saucepan over medium-low heat, add all ingredients and simmer for 30 minutes. Don't let the mixture boil.

2. Remove from the heat and let cool for 10 minutes.

3. Remove the peels, cinnamon sticks, and cloves and pour the mixture into heatproof serving glasses.

4. Halve the apple and cut it into thin wedges.

5. Garnish each glass with an apple wedge and serve.

Decorations

"Ever afterwards the young man could recollect individually each part of the service of that bright Christmas morning, and the trifling occurrences which took place as its minutes slowly drew along; the duties of that day dividing themselves by a complete line from the services of other times. The tunes they that morning essayed remained with him for years, apart from all others; also the text; also the appearance of the layer of dust upon the capitals of the piers; that the holly-bough in the chancel archway was hung a little out of the centre—all the ideas, in short, that creep into the mind when reason is only exercising its lowest activity through the eye."

—From *Under the Greenwood Tree*
by Thomas Hardy, 1872

HRISTMAS DECORATIONS vary from country to country, but the tradition of adorning homes during the winter solstice dates back thousands of years. In the Northern Hemisphere, the solstice takes place most often on the 21st of December but occasionally on the 20th or 22nd. That first day of winter contains the fewest hours of daylight in the year. In the Southern Hemisphere, the date marks the summer solstice, and the day contains the most daylight.

TREES

As with many seasonal traditions, the practice of honouring a tree during the winter festival predates Christianity. In antiquity, Romans and Celts decorated their homes with evergreens to symbolise the fruitful return of spring and summer. In the Germanic lands of medieval Europe, many Christians decorated what they called paradise trees. They hung fruit, especially apples, on fir trees to represent the Garden of Eden. The practice took place on the feast day of Saints Adam and Eve, observed on the 24th of December. As a result, the paradise tree became emblematic of the Christmas season there.

Many European countries have records of trees being decorated and then burnt in a ceremonial blaze to mark the winter solstice. Tallinn in Estonia and Riga in Latvia both claim credit as the first city, in the 1400s, to decorate a public Christmas tree. German theologian and priest Martin Luther receives credit for bringing the first Christmas tree inside the home. The story goes that, at Christmastime, he was walking through some woods when stars shining through fir trees mesmerised him. The beautiful sight reminded him of the star that guided the Magi to the baby Jesus, so he cut down a fir tree, dragged it home, and adorned it with candles so his family could experience the same effect that he had witnessed.

DECORATIONS

By the early 1600s, decorating a Christmas tree inside the home had become a popular activity in Germany: "At Christmas, they set up fir trees in the parlours of Strasbourg and hang thereon roses cut from many-coloured paper, apples, wafers, gold foil, sweets, etc.," according to an anonymous record from 1605. This practice spread throughout Europe and eventually across the world.

Queen Charlotte's New Tradition

In 1761, Princess Sophia Charlotte of Mecklenburg-Strelitz married King George III of Britain and Ireland, the third Hanoverian monarch to rule the islands. From 1762 to 1783, Queen Charlotte gave birth to fifteen children, and every Christmas the princes and princesses celebrated the traditions that their mother had enjoyed as a girl. Initially, those customs involved decorating yew branches and placing them atop presents for the children. In December 1798, English poet Samuel Taylor Coleridge visited the duchy of Mecklenburg-Strelitz, where the queen had grown up, and later wrote to his wife of what he had witnessed:

> On the evening before Christmas Day, one of the parlours is lighted up by the children, into which the parents must not go; a great yew bough is fastened on the table at a little distance from the wall, a multitude of little tapers are fixed in the bough . . . and coloured paper etc. hangs and flutters from the twigs. Under this bough the children lay out the presents they mean for their parents, still concealing in their pockets what they intend for each other. Then the parents are introduced, and each presents his little gift; they then bring out the remainder one by one from their pockets, and present them with kisses and embraces.

That sweet tradition eventually led to the queen decorating a whole tree with help from her ladies-in-waiting. The exact date of the first occasion remains unknown, but in 1800 the queen shared the idea with a group of children whose parents worked for the royal household. At a Christmas party at Windsor Castle, the children entered the queen's drawing room to behold a decorated tree—a yew tree in a pot—glittering with candles and presents. John Watkins, who attended the party and later penned a biography of the queen, described the sight: "From the branches . . . hung bunches of sweetmeats, almonds and raisins in papers, fruits and toys, most tastefully arranged; the whole illuminated by small wax candles. . . . After the company had walked round and admired the tree, each child obtained a portion of the sweets it bore, together with a toy, and then all returned home quite delighted." Almost at once, members of the royal household and those close to the royal family adopted this new custom, but several decades passed before most Britons outside aristocratic circles even heard about Christmas trees.

Princess Alexandrina's Christmas Tree

Nevertheless, the tradition of the Christmas tree continued in the royal household. In 1832, Princess Alexandrina, age 13, was living in Kensington Palace with her mother, the duchess of Kent and Strathearn, and wrote in her diary on the 24th of December 1832:

> After dinner we went upstairs. I then saw Flora, the
> dog which Sir John was going to give Mamma. . . .
> We then went into the drawing-room near the dining-
> room. After Mamma had rung a bell three times we
> went in. There were two large round tables on which
> were placed two trees hung with lights and sugar

ornaments. All the presents being placed round the
tree. I had one table for myself.

If none of her uncles sired a legitimate child, this once-obscure princess, now heir presumptive to King William IV, stood to inherit the
British throne, which she did on the 20th of June 1837. She chose
her second name, Victoria, as her regnal name.

Queen Victoria's Christmas Trees

In February 1840, Queen Victoria married Albert of Saxe-Coburg
and Gotha. Later that year, Prince Albert ordered spruce and firs
from his homeland for Christmas in Britain. At the end of the following year, the queen wrote in her diary, "Today I have two children
of my own . . . who, they know not why, are full of happy wonder at
the German Christmas tree and its radiant candles." Soon, newspapers were reporting on the royal family's seasonal celebrations,
including their Christmas trees, which included three artificial fir
trees more than eight feet tall and made of

> metal covered with natural leaves . . . each beauti-
> fully ornamented with 72 wax lights, appended to the
> branches. . . . The stems to which the branches and
> lights were affixed, were of real fir. One of the trees
> was entirely frosted over to resemble icicles of snow.
> To the branches of each were suspended an immense
> quantity of bon bons (for presentation to the company)
> contained in small boxes and cases . . . richly and elab-
> orately ornamented. One of these trees was for her Maj-
> esty, another for the Prince consort, and the third for
> the Duchess of Kent. There was also a fourth, similarly

illuminated and ornamented, and festooned with bon
bons, for his Royal Highness the Prince of Wales.

In 1848, the *Morning Post* reported

A Christmas tree is annually prepared by her Majesty's command, for the Royal Children. The tree
employed for this festive purpose is a young fir, around
eight feet high, and has six tiers of branches. On each
tier or branch are arranged a dozen wax tapers. Pen-
dant from the branches are elegant trays, baskets,
bonbonnières, and other receptacles for sweetmeats,
of the most varied kind, and of all forms, colours, and
degrees of beauty. Fancy cakes, gilt gingerbread, and
eggs filled with sweetmeats are also suspended by var-
iously coloured ribands from the branches. The tree,
which stands upon a table covered with white damask,
is supported at the root by piles of sweets of a larger
kind, and by toys and dolls of all description. . . . The
name of each recipient is affixed to the doll, bonbon,
or other present intended for it. . . . On the summit of
the tree stands the small figure of an angel, with out-
stretched wings, holding in each hand a wreath. Similar trees are arranged . . . for the Duchess of Kent and
the royal household. These trees are objects of much
interest to all visitors at the Castle, from Christmas
Eve, when they are first set up, until Twelfth Night,
when they are finally removed. They are not accessible
to the curiosity of the public, but her Majesty's visitors
accompany the Queen from room to room to inspect
them when they are illuminated.

The Christmas Tree at Windsor Castle by J. L. Williams, 1848

That year, the prince consort also sent decorated Christmas trees to Eton College and to the army barracks near Windsor Castle. Because newspapers and the public had shown such interest in this custom, Prince Albert decided that people should witness the tradition with more than just a description. In December 1848, the *Illustrated London News* published a special seasonal supplement containing a drawing of the royal parents and children standing beside a decorated fir tree. This image introduced the Christmas tree to many Britons and people living in other countries where the newspaper circulated. Suddenly Christmas trees appeared in homes across the anglophone world. Those who couldn't afford to buy a whole tree craftily made one of gathered twigs, evergreen branches, paper, rags, ribbons, and a lot of imagination.

Queen Victoria's Christmas tree at Windsor Castle, 1850

In 1850, the queen decorated her Christmas tree at Windsor Castle with wax candles and fake snow, surrounding it with sumptuous gifts. She also commissioned watercolour artist James Roberts to depict it, which further popularised the custom around the world. In 1853, the first year of his presidency, Franklin Pierce decorated an evergreen tree in the gardens of the White House. In 1889, President Benjamin Harrison brought the tree inside the White House for decorating, just as Martin Luther had done centuries earlier.

Christmas Baubles

In the late 1500s, in Lauscha, current-day Germany, Hans Greiner innovated glass decorations for ornamenting tees. Often in the shapes of nuts and fruits, these ornaments, silvered inside to glitter brightly, reflected the light of candles glowing from the branches of Christmas trees. This decorative tradition soon made its way to the rest of Europe. In the 1880s, Frank Woolworth's eponymous five-and-dime store was expanding in America. He visited Germany and, in Lauscha, encountered Greiner's Christmas baubles. Woolworth imported the baubles to the USA, which helped make his fortune and create an enduring seasonal tradition.

WREATHS

From the centuries-old practice of bringing evergreen branches into the home, decorative wreaths evolved, at first to hold Advent candles. By the Middle Ages, churches had adopted the practice widely, with many parish records showing entries for purchasing evergreens, especially holly and ivy, for the season. We don't know who created the first Christmas wreath or when, but hanging one on a door became a fashionable practice in the Victorian age.

Advent Wreaths

In the 1500s, Germanic Lutherans began the ecclesiastical tradition of evergreen Advent wreaths. These wreaths contained either four or five candles. If four, each one, usually red, marked a successive Sunday preceding Christmas and represented an aspect of the Advent tradition: prophecy, Bethlehem, shepherds, and angels. If a fifth candle appeared, usually white, observers lighted that Christ candle on Christmas Eve or Christmas Day. Records indicate that Johann Wichern, a pastor in Hamburg, created the modern Advent wreath for use in secular settings in 1839 by adding candles to the wheel of a cart laid horizontally.

MISTLETOE

As with so many Victorian Christmas decorations, bringing mistletoe into the home has ancient origins. In pagan times, people used the plant to ward off evil spirits and signify love and friendship. The ancient Romans ascribed properties of love, peace, and sympathy to it, and early Christians incorporated it into their sacred celebrations. For centuries, celebrants at York Minster—founded in AD 627, making it one of the oldest cathedrals in England—have used mistletoe in their festive celebrations. The priest blesses a bunch of mistletoe and hangs it above the altar, a tradition echoing an early practice of using mistletoe at Christmas to pardon the sins of those seeking forgiveness. From this long association with forgiveness and friendship, a parallel ancient tradition holds that, when people enter a household, they offer the kiss of friendship to the householder under a bunch of mistletoe.

By the Victorian era, mistletoe formed part of a Christmas courtship ritual known as a kissing bunch. If a woman was standing under mistletoe, a lucky man nearby could kiss her without

refusal. In the 1800s, the tradition included the rules that
each kiss required removing
a berry and that the kissing had to stop when the
bunch held no more berries.
Not surprisingly, people in
strict religious households
banned mistletoe from their
seasonal decorations.

In 1835, Charles Dickens
wrote "A Christmas Dinner"
(also called "Christmas Festivities"), his first seasonal
short story. In it, a grandfa-
ther tells his grandchildren
that, as a boy, he had kissed their grandmother under some mistletoe. *The Pickwick Papers*, published in 1837, also mentions the
holiday plant.

> According to annual custom on Christmas Eve . . .
> From the centre of the ceiling of this kitchen, old
> Wardle had just suspended, with his own hands,
> a huge branch of mistletoe, and this same branch
> of mistletoe instantaneously gave rise to a scene of
> general and most delightful struggling and confusion;
> in the midst of which, Mr. Pickwick, with a gallantry
> that would have done honour to a descendant of Lady
> Tollimglower herself, took the old lady by the hand,
> led her beneath the mystic branch, and saluted her in
> all courtesy and decorum.

CHRISTMAS CRACKERS

In 1848, Thomas Smith, a British confectioner, visited Paris, where he saw bonbons wrapped in twists of paper. He used the idea for his own Christmas confectionery containing sugared almonds. Over the next few years, he introduced new ideas to the presentation. Inside the paper casing, he inserted little mottos alongside the nuts. The idea proved incredibly popular, so he patented his innovation and continued working on it. He added a rod of stiff paper to the casing, reportedly to re-create the sound of a log fire. When pulled

apart, the stiff paper crackled satisfyingly. By the 1860s, Smith had perfected the "crack," which gave the item its name, by using silver fulminate snaps to create a bang when opening it. He also swapped the sugared almonds for little gifts for adults and children. In the 1870s, he added paper hats to the parcels, giving us all the components of the modern-day Christmas cracker.

Many cultures consider it bad luck to leave Christmas decorations up beyond Twelfth Night, but other parts of the world always leave them in place until Candlemas. English poet Robert Herrick wrote this short poem about the superstition associated with leaving them up after Candlemas, a fitting end to our survey of Victorian Christmas decorations.

Ceremony upon Candlemas Eve

Down with the rosemary, and so
Down with the bays and mistletoe;
Down with the holly, ivy, all
Wherewith ye dress'd the Christmas hall;
That so the superstitious find
No one least branch there left behind;
For look, how many leaves there be
Neglected there, maids, trust to me,
So many goblins you shall see.

CHRISTMAS CRAFTS

Christmas Tree Decorations

A real fir, pine, or spruce tree for Christmas imparts a wonderful, seasonal scent to the home. If you already have or prefer to use an artificial tree, it remains well within Victorian Christmas tradition. Remember, Queen Victoria herself displayed artificial fir trees in 1840. Whatever kind of tree you have, the fun lies in decorating it.

Dried Fruit

Slices of dried apples and oranges make for pretty decorations and add even more seasonal scent to a room. It's also super easy to slice them into bells, snowflakes, snowmen, stars, stockings, and other holiday shapes.

apples and/or oranges
kitchen scissors

spices such as whole cloves and/or ground cinnamon (optional)
ribbon, string, or twine

1. Preheat the oven to its lowest temperature.

2. Peel the fruits and cut them into ¼-inch (6.5 mm) slices. If creating shapes, do so now.

3. Punch a small hole at the top of each slice.

4. On a baking sheet lined with a wire oven rack or parchment paper, lay the slices flat.

5. If using spices, stud each of the slices with a few cloves and/or sprinkle with ground cinnamon.

6. Bake the slices for 3 to 4 hours, remove from the oven, and let cool to room temperature.

7. Thread the slices through the punched holes with ribbon, string, or twine.

8. Hang them on the tree.

SUGAR PLUMS

Recorded at the wedding of King Henry IV of England to Princess Joan of Navarre in 1403, "sugar plums" for centuries referred to an array of candied fruits created by sugar panning. That laborious method made them an expensive commodity. But in the 1860s, producers innovated more cost-effective ways to create them, including rotating pans and steam heat. Still, most Victorian children didn't have access to the sugary treats prevalent today, so sugar-coated dried fruits on the tree made for a special, tasty tradition. This simple recipe calls for pitted plums preserved in syrup and *lots* of extra sugar. If you can't find preserved plums, use any similar fruit, such as apricots or figs, in syrup.

plums, pitted and preserved in syrup

granulated sugar
baking sheet
thread

1. Preheat the oven to its lowest temperature.

2. Into a rimmed baking sheet, spread a layer of sugar and, into a small bowl, pour more sugar.

3. Let the excess syrup drain off the plums and back into the jar.

4. Swirl one of the plums in the bowl of sugar until fully coated.

5. Place it onto the prepared baking tray and repeat with all the plums.

continues ❊-

European plum

6. Let them rest for 10 minutes. If the sugar coating soaks completely into the syrup, roll them in the bowl of sugar again and let them rest for 10 more minutes.

7. Bake until the sugar coating dries, about 2 hours.

8. Remove from the oven and let cool to room temperature.

9. Tie them with a loop of thread and hang them on your Christmas tree.

Salt Dough Ornaments

If you prefer to eat your apples, oranges, and plums, you can have lots of fun baking ornaments from scratch with a few simple ingredients. Consider using cookie cutters to create bells, snowflakes, snowmen, stars, stockings, and other shapes.

1 cup (120 g) all-purpose flour

½ cup (135 g) salt

½ cup (125 ml) warm water

food colouring (optional)

parchment paper

rolling pin or heavy, cylindrical glass

cookie cutters (optional)

skewer or toothpick

cranberries, cloves, pine needles, rosemary, or similar adornments (optional)

ribbon, string, or twine

1. Preheat the oven to its lowest temperature.

2. In a medium mixing bowl, combine the flour, salt, and water. Stir until a dough forms.

3. If colouring your dough, divide it into different containers and add the colouring—such as gold, green, silver, and red—to each container. Mix and, wearing gloves, knead to incorporate the colour fully.

continues ❧

4. Line a baking sheet with parchment paper.

5. With a rolling pin or heavy, cylindrical glass, roll out the dough to ¼-inch (6.5 mm) thick.

6. Use cookie cutters to create seasonal shapes or form them by hand. For example, three thin strands of green dough braided together and looped into a circle will look like a little Christmas wreath, to which you can add a small red bow.

7. With a skewer or toothpick, punch a small hole in the top of each ornament.

8. If decorating the shapes further, stud them with cranberries, cloves, pine needles, rosemary, or similar.

9. Bake until firm, 2 to 3 hours, remove from the oven, and let cool to room temperature.

10. Thread the ornaments through the punched holes with ribbon, string, or twine.

11. Hang them on the tree.

ACORN GARLAND

You can create a special garland by painting acorns different colours and stringing them together. If you have them in seasonal colours, consider using old bottles of nail varnish to paint them in festive patterns.

acorns, foraged
  or store-bought
aluminium foil

craft paints and small paint
  brush or nail varnish/polish
hot glue gun or small drill
string or twine

1. If foraging acorns, avoid any with holes in them, which likely contain insects that you don't want to bring home!

2. Preheat the oven to 225°F (110°C; gas mark ¼).

3. Rinse the acorns in cold water and gently pat them dry.

4. On a foil-lined baking sheet, bake the acorns for 1 hour.

5. Remove from the oven and let them cool to room temperature.

6. If any of the tops fall off, glue them back on and let the glue dry completely.

7. Paint the bottoms of the acorns with the craft paints or nail polish/varnish, leaving the tops their natural colour. Let them dry completely.

8. If using a hot glue gun, dab a small bead of hot glue to the back of an acorn cap and attach the string or twine to it. If using a drill, choose a bit slightly thicker than the string or twine. Below the cap, drill straight through the centre of the painted acorn.

9. Leave about 12 inches (30 cm) of string or twine before the first acorn and after the last one to allow you to tie the garland in place.

10. Wrap the garland around your tree, hang it from your mantel, or display it in another festive location.

FABRIC DECORATIONS

This method offers a great way to upcycle fabric scraps or to repurpose holiday-themed fabrics. Alternatively, if you knit or crochet, stitch seasonal shapes to hang on the tree.

1. If you sew, cut two identical shapes—bells, snowflakes, snowmen, stars, stockings, and so on—from a piece of fabric.

2. Sew three-quarters of the edges together to create a pocket.

3. Fill it with seasonal spices, such as whole cloves, nutmeg seeds, or dried orange peel.

4. Sew the last quarter of the ornament shut and trim with a ribbon loop for hanging.

FOIL SHAPES

In the late 1800s, manufacturers introduced foil made from tin for sale to the public. It instantly became popular as a Christmas decoration. Children made little tinfoil sculptures and placed them on the branches of Christmas trees, where they reflected the candlelight and made the trees sparkle even more. After World War II, aluminium replaced tin in the marketplace, but you can cut and shape aluminium foil into seasonal shapes to decorate your Christmas tree.

GOLDEN WALNUTS

Popular in the Victorian age, these gilded beauties serve as eye-catching ornaments and little presents.

whole walnuts	glue
paper	red ribbon or string (optional)
pen	gold paint or gold leaf
small gifts or trinkets	

1. Carefully crack open the walnuts, keeping the shells intact and keeping each pair of shells together.

2. Remove the nutmeats and store them in an airtight jar or eat them.

3. On a small slip of paper, write a motto or kind holiday message. Fold the slip and place it inside a walnut shell.

4. Into the opposite shell, place a little gift or trinket.

5. If hanging the walnuts from your tree, carefully glue the two halves of the shell back together with a loop of red ribbon or string held between the top of the two shells. Let dry completely.

6. Paint or gild the shells and let dry completely.

7. Hang the gilded shells on the Christmas tree or place elsewhere around your home, such as on a mantelpiece or dangling from a kissing bunch (page 89). For a different presentation, omit the ribbon and pile the gilded walnuts in a decorative bowl displayed prominently in your home.

PAPER CHAINS

In the 1800s, many Victorian children collected old newspapers and other wastepaper to make paper chains, a popular Christmas decoration. Any reasonably stiff paper will do.

paper   scissors
ruler   glue
pencil

1. Measure, mark, and cut the paper into strips of roughly the same size, such as ½ inch by 4 inches (12 cm) by 100 cm.

2. To make each link of the chain unique, decorate the strips of paper before fashioning them into chains.

3. Dab glue onto one end of the first strip of paper, loop it into a circle to glue the opposite end to it, and hold the two ends of the loop together until the glue dries. While you wait, consider playing a Victorian word game, such as I Love My Love (page 131) or The Parson's Cat (page 132).

4. Dab glue on one end of a second strip of paper, thread it through the first loop, form another loop, and secure the end until it dries.

5. Continue until you make a chain, which can stretch as long as your paper supply or imagination allows!

House Decorations

For the holiday season, you can decorate more than just a tree. The crafts in this section will infuse your whole home with Christmas spirit.

Christmas Wreaths

In 1855, Alexander Parkes invented the first fabricated plastic in Birmingham, but the Victorians didn't have plastic decorations. Take a leaf from their book and make a natural wreath the old-fashioned way.

willow or hazel branches, strong creepers, thin cane, or floral wire

gardening twine

greenery

decorations such as acorns, cinnamon sticks, dried fruit, flowers (fresh, dried, or paper), Golden Walnuts (page 85), pine cones, ribbons, or small wooden toys

1. Create a circle from the branches, creepers, cane, or floral wire. For a small wreath, 1 foot (300 cm) in diameter, you'll need about 3 feet (1 metre) of material—more for a larger wreath. Secure the circle with gardening twine.

2. Wrap local greenery neatly around the circle to create a lush, thick base for adding decorations.

3. Determine which point of the wreath will serve as the top. Make a loop of gardening twine and secure it there. The finished wreath may weigh a lot, so secure it strongly. Depending on the weight of the decorations, you may want to double or triple the loop for added support.

4. Attach the decorations with more gardening twine.

5. Hang the wreath securely on a door or wall.

POMANDERS

Originally used in the Middle Ages for medicinal purposes, pomanders add beautiful holiday scent to any room, Victorian or otherwise!

ribbon	**toothpick**
orange	**whole cloves**
thumbtacks	

1. From top to bottom, wrap the ribbon around the orange, then tie it around again so the ribbon forms a cross. Fasten the ribbon in place with a couple of thumbtacks pushed through the ribbon and into the orange.

2. At the top of the orange, tie the ribbon into a bow. If you plan on hanging the pomander, add a loop above the bow.

3. Use the toothpick to make holes for the cloves. Consider making patterns or shapes.

4. Into each hole, firmly push a clove so that only the head remains visible.

5. Place or hang the pomander where its seasonal scent can fill the room.

KISSING BUNCHES

This is the proper name for the gatherings of mistletoe hung at Christmastime under which to steal cheeky kisses. If ingested, mistletoe berries can poison children and pets, so hang your kissing bunch where fallen berries won't pose a hazard, or consider wrapping it in a thin mesh covering.

mistletoe

ribbon

evergreens or dried flowers (optional)

1. Tie the stalks of a bunch of mistletoe together with a length of ribbon, being careful not to damage the leaves or berries.

2. Thread a second ribbon through the first, make a loop, and secure its ends. This loop will allow you to hang the kissing bunch.

3. If you have only a little mistletoe, add evergreens or dried flowers to the kissing bunch, but make sure that the mistletoe remains visible.

4. Tie thinner ribbons to the mistletoe bunch so they hang down and flutter whenever the door opens.

5. Hang the kissing bunch inside the front door to greet your guests as they arrive.

CHRISTMAS CRACKERS

Set on the dining table, one for each person, these festive decorations make a fun start to Christmas dinner. The paper needs to tear easily, so use wrapping paper, crepe paper, or similar. For the tubes, cut down the cardboard roll from wrapping paper or paper towels, or use toilet rolls. If you can't find cracker snaps, write BANG! on a piece of paper that will flutter down from the pulled cracker. In addition to the items below, you can add other decorations of choice, such as pictures cut from last year's Christmas cards, ribbons, buttons, or paper flowers.

ruler	paper
cardboard tubes	pen
colourful paper	tape
scissors	raffia or ribbon
glue	paper hats
cracker snaps	small gifts or sweets

1. Measure the length of an individual cracker tube and roll out three times that length of paper for wrapping it. Each piece of paper should be wide enough to wrap around the tube completely.

2. Depending on the desired length of each cracker, cut each tube into 2 or 3 sections, making sure not to squash the cardboard.

3. In the centre of either end of the paper, dab a small blob of glue. Don't use too much glue, or the cracker won't break. Lay the ends of the snaps in the glue and let it dry completely.

4. While you wait, write mottos, messages, or jokes on slips of paper, one for each cracker.

5. When the glue has dried, roll the tube sections in the paper and tape the paper into place.

6. At one end of the cracker, twist the overhanging paper closed and tie it with raffia or ribbon.

7. Into the open end of the cracker, insert a paper hat, a motto or joke, and small gifts or sweets.

8. At the open end, twist the overhanging paper closed and tie it with raffia or ribbon.

9. Decorate the paper any way you like. You can write the recipients' names on the crackers or add name tags to ensure everyone receives the intended gifts—especially useful if making crackers for different age groups.

10. When the time comes to open them, pair up and pull at both ends simultaneously to activate the cracker snap and release the gifts.

CHRISTMAS CANDLES

Lighting candles, such as those in an Advent wreath (page 72), has a long association with Christmas, symbolising Jesus Christ as the light of the world. Over time, the oil lamps of antiquity evolved into candles, so this tradition connects Christmas celebrations not only with ancient pagan festivals but also with other festivals of light from all over the world, including Diwali, Eid, Hanukkah, the Lantern Festival, Tazaungdaing, and other celebrations. For this activity, select a candle—coloured and/or seasonally scented if you like—and pray or meditate on the blessings of the holiday.

YULE LOGS

The word *Yule* originally referred to a pre-Christian Scandinavian festival celebrating the winter solstice, and fire formed an essential part of the observance. A family searched for a large piece of wood, which could consist of an entire tree. From it, they lit a fire, carefully guarding it and keeping it burning for the twelve days of Yule. Many households kept the remains of the Yule log for a year, using the remnants of the previous year's log to kindle the next year's fire.

If you have a working fireplace, you can buy or, better yet, forage your own Yule log. As you light it, reflect on the previous year

and what you wish for the year ahead. If you have the appropriate storage space, save a few pieces or branches of the log to kindle next year's fire. If you don't have a fireplace, consider watching a video of a Yule log burning, seasonally available on certain channels, many streaming platforms, or any video-hosting website. Instead of burning or watching one, you might consider making a household activity of baking and eating a Chocolate Yule Log (page 49) with Christmas dinner.

SCENTED FIRE

If you have a wood-burning fireplace, chiminea, or barbecue— depending on your Christmas climate—you can add seasonal scent to your home or garden with one or more of the following items. If burning pine cones, always use mature, dried cones. Young, fresh ones can cause the fire to spit.

cinnamon sticks	**dried oranges**
citrus fruit peels	**dried pine cones**
dried apples	**dried rosemary**
dried bay leaves	**dried sage**

Activities

"The Christmas festival has languished . . . but never has been, and never will be, extinct. The stately forms of its celebration in high places have long since (and, in all probability, forever) passed away. . . . But the spirit of the season yet survives . . . while the ancient sports and ceremonies are widely scattered, many of them have retreated into obscure places, and some perhaps are lost. Still, however, this period of commemoration is everywhere a merry time."

—From *The Book of Christmas*
by Thomas Hervey, 1837

OR MANY centuries and for many people, Christmas functioned as a working day like any other. The Victorian emphasis on its religious and social significance, however, transformed it, eventually, into an international holiday on which few people had to work. Victorians marked or filled the day in a wide variety of ways.

CHRISTMAS CARDS

Early in Queen Victoria's reign, 1843 marked a turning point in how Britain and much of the wider world celebrated Christmas. That year saw the creation of the first commercial Christmas card. At the time, convention dictated that people send long, handwritten Christmas letters, but Henry Cole, a perennially busy civil servant in London, simply didn't have the time, however. He asked John Callcott Horsley, an artist friend, to design a card for him. The card, which showed the Cole family celebrating the holiday, offered the perfect way to send the season's greetings without writing numerous, lengthy letters.

On the 17th of December 1843, Cole recorded in his diary, "In the ev[enin]g Horsley came & brought his design for Christmas cards." The design consisted of three drawings. The middle contained a sketch of three generations of Cole's family raising their glasses in a toast to Christmas. On either side appeared images of people giving gifts of food and warm clothing to the poor. Underneath, a banner declared: A MERRY CHRISTMAS AND A HAPPY NEW YEAR TO YOU.

The card proved controversial, however. Cole and his wife had eight children, plus grandchildren, and the Christmas card depicted some of the young ones drinking wine. Members of the Temperance Society voiced their outrage. Furious letters to newspapers lambasted Cole for promoting the giving of alcohol to children.

Portrait of Henry Cole by James Tissot, from *Vanity Fair*, 1871

Contentious and expensive to produce, the card flopped. Five years passed before someone else tried one. Created by artist William Maw Egley, this second card featured several different festive scenes, including ballet dancers, family parties, a Christmas dinner table, and people giving alms to the poor.

It took roughly a decade for Cole's time-saving experiment to become a recognisable part of seasonal celebrations. By the mid-1850s, publishers were producing Christmas cards in bulk and selling them through stationery shops and newspaper advertisements. The Christmas card received further boosts in 1870 with the implementation of an affordable postal service; in 1875, when Louis Prang introduced Christmas cards to the American market; and in the 1880s, when printing costs fell, making cards more affordable for the masses.

The first Christmas card, 1843

Depictions of Santa Claus

In 1821, the first known illustration of Santa Claus appeared in *The Children's Friend* by Arthur Stansbury. Christmas cards, as they grew in popularity, happily adopted the jolly personification of the holiday. In the 1860s, *Harper's Weekly* magazine commissioned Thomas Nast, a German American illustrator, to draw the cover for a Christmas edition of the publication. Nast's enormously influential political cartoons had attracted the attention of President Abraham Lincoln, who, according to legend, suggested the theme for the holiday illustration. The 3rd of January 1863 cover of *Harper's* shows an image of Santa Claus dressed in the stars and stripes of the American flag, giving presents from his sleigh to Union troops. In a second illustration in the magazine, flying reindeer draw Santa Claus through the sky. These iconic illustrations—the beginning of Nast's long career of drawing Santa Claus—helped turn St. Nick into the iconic image that endures today.

For much of the 1800s, most American children believed that

Santa Claus lived in Manhattan (or on the moon). As development spread and the wild spaces of Manhattan disappeared, that belief became increasingly hard to hold. Children were writing letters to Santa, which meant that he needed a proper address, so Nast and the editor of *Harper's* contemplated Santa's ideal home. It made good sense to locate him somewhere that reindeer lived and that had perpetual snow. On the 29th of December 1866, the magazine published Nast's cartoons of Santa Claus at home at the North Pole, an unpopulated region that explorers hadn't reached yet, making it the perfect place for St. Nick to live without fear of unwanted visitors.

For centuries, St. Nicholas/Father Christmas/Santa Claus didn't wear the red and white outfit that he does today. In England, he usually wore green robes, harking back to the Green Man, an ancient figure from British mythology. Often carved into the architecture of medieval churches, the Green Man had a beard of leaves sprouting from his face, and foliage often surrounded him. The tradition likely derives from medieval tales of Seth, the third son of Adam and Eve, who placed seeds in the mouth of his dead father. From one of those seeds grew a tree that ultimately provided the wood for the cross of the crucifixion. As such, the Green Man represents rebirth and resurrection, which of course resonates with the religious meaning of Christmas. In Charles Dickens's *A Christmas Carol*, illustrator John Leech depicted the Ghost of Christmas Present with a large beard and wearing flowing robes of green and white.

From the 1870s onwards, some Christmas cards show Santa in his now signature red robes, and in the early 1900s, he was wearing other colours, including blue, purple, and brown. But the red and white costume became ubiquitous thanks to advertisements of the 1930s using Santa as an extension of the brand design for Coca-Cola.

CHRISTMAS STORIES

Before the Victorian age began, most authors who wrote seasonal stories did so for children. In 1843, however, *A Christmas Carol* changed literary history, igniting a craze for Christmas stories written for adults, which hasn't waned. That novella remains the most famous in the genre, but many authors in addition to Dickens made a good living writing seasonal tales.

"Nußknacker und Mausekönig" (Nutcracker and Mouse King) by Ernst Hoffman, 1816

This now-iconic Christmas story served as the inspiration for *The Nutcracker* ballet, but the original tale runs much darker. A fairy tale, it satirises the cruelty, depression, greed, and social hierarchies of society, albeit with a happy ending. On Christmas Eve, Marie (not Clara, as she is named in the ballet) and her brother, Fritz, eagerly await the arrival of Drosselmeyer, their one-eyed godfather and a maker of curious toys. Drosselmeyer brings a grand mechanical castle for them, but an "ugly" nutcracker catches Marie's attention.

That night, Marie stays awake and witnesses toys come alive to fight a fierce band of mice ruled by the Mouse King. She sustains injuries in the battle, but her family members don't believe her explanation. Drosselmeyer believes her, however, admitting that the Nutcracker is his cursed nephew. At the end of the story, she unwittingly breaks the curse, accepts the restored nephew's proposal of marriage, and becomes queen of the doll kingdom.

In 1844, Alexandre Dumas adapted Hoffman's story, making the plot less gothic and more palatable for parents to share with children. Russian composer Pyotr Tchaikovsky used the gentler

"Jo was the first to wake in the gray dawn of Christmas morning. No stockings hung at the fireplace, and for a moment she felt as much disappointed as she did long ago, when her little sock fell down because it was crammed so full of goodies. Then she remembered her mother's promise and, slipping her hand under her pillow, drew out a little crimson-covered book. She knew it very well, for it was that beautiful old story of the best life ever lived, and Jo felt that it was a true guidebook for any pilgrim going on a long journey. She woke Meg with a 'Merry Christmas,' and bade her see what was under her pillow. A green-covered book appeared, with the same picture inside, and a few words written by their mother, which made their one present very precious in their eyes. Presently Beth and Amy woke to rummage and find their little books also, one dove-colored, the other blue, and all sat looking at and talking about them, while the east grew rosy with the coming day."

—From *Little Women* by Louisa Alcott, 1869

Dumas version to create his *Nutcracker* ballet, which premiered in Saint Petersburg in December 1892.

The Keeping of Christmas at Bracebridge Hall by Washington Irving, 1822

In 1815, Washington Irving travelled from America to Europe in search of work and to visit his sister Sarah and her husband, who lived in Birmingham. While there, Irving wrote nostalgically about how Christmas was changing: "Nothing in England exercises a more delightful spell over my imagination, than the lingerings of the holiday customs and rural games of former times. . . . I regret to say that they are daily growing more and more faint, being gradually worn away by time—but still more obliterated by modern fashion. . . . Many of the games and ceremonials of Christmas have entirely disappeared."

The narrator of *The Keeping of Christmas at Bracebridge Hall*, like its author, is travelling around England. On a snowy Christmas Eve, feeling lonely at a country inn, he encounters Frank Bracebridge, a young man. Bracebridge invites the narrator to stay at his family home (modelled on Birmingham's Aston Hall) for Christmas. Age 10 when the story appeared, Dickens read and enjoyed it, eventually counting Irving amongst his favourite writers.

"Account of a Visit from St. Nicholas," 1823

In 1823, the *Troy Sentinel* newspaper published this anonymous poem with the famous first couplet:

'Twas the night before Christmas, when all thro' the house, not a creature was stirring, not even a mouse.

Clement Moore, a Manhattan landholder and linguist, later received credit for writing it. In recent years, some scholars have questioned his authorship, but the manuscript sent to the *Troy Sentinel* hasn't survived, so the question remains unanswered. Many literary historians continue to attribute it to Moore.

"Ночь перед Рождеством" (The Night before Christmas) by Nikolai Gogol, 1832

Born in Ukraine, then part of the Russian Empire, Nikolai Gogol famously introduced the grotesque and surrealist techniques to fiction in short stories such as "The Diary of a Madman" and "The Overcoat," his play *The Government Inspector*, and novels *Dead Souls* and *Taras Bulba*. In this short story, set on Christmas Eve, Vakula, the village blacksmith and an artist, has depicted a devil as ugly. In retribution, the angry devil steals the moon, roaming the village with it in his pocket, determined to exact his revenge on the blacksmith. Equally determined to beat the devil, Vakula also wants to win the love of Oksana, the daughter of a Cossack, who until now has ignored him. All the while, Solokha, a witch, flies above the town, watching over her son, the blacksmith. Not your typical Christmas story!

A Christmas Carol by Charles Dickens, 1843

In the 1840s, Britain was suffering an economic depression later called the Hungry Forties. Dickens wrote *A Christmas Carol* in response to the poverty all around him. Most people think of Ebenezer Scrooge and the Christmas ghosts as the main characters, but Dickens intended to bring the poor children—in particular Tiny Tim and Ignorance and Want, the two children who appear with the Ghost of Christmas Present—to the forefront of the book. Dickens wrote to a friend that his novella would strike "a sledgehammer blow" on behalf of "the poor man's child."

Always a popular holiday in the Dickens household, Christmas

offered occasion for parties, music, and dancing. Others outside the family didn't feel as keen on the season, however. When Dickens told Chapman and Hall, his publishers, that he had an idea for a novella about the holiday, they expressed their scepticism, not thinking the subject commercially appealing. He held firm, so they insisted that he cover a large percentage of the production costs, meaning that, in essence, Dickens partially self-published the novella.

Released on the 19th of December 1843, *A Christmas Carol* became an instant success, selling through its first print run of 6,000 copies in just five days. On the 23rd of December 1843, the editor of the *Bristol Mercury* newspaper noted that

> Mr. Charles Dickens has just published a "Christmas Carol in prose," the object of which is to show that the truest way of enjoying your own Christmas is, for those who have the power, to take steps to add, according to their means, to the pleasure of some other person's Christmas. Mr. Dickens's heart seems as right as his head, and there can be no doubt that, in the present instance, his philosophy is sound. It would therefore be well for us all, as individuals, to endeavour to do some little good in our several walks of life (and the opportunities are ample), and so be the medium, at the present pre-eminently charitable season, of diffusing those comforts without which, to the poor, there can be no "merry Christmas"!

Since its first publication, the book has never gone out of print. It created a new category: Christmas stories for adults; a new subgenre: the Christmas ghost story; and reinvigorated many other industries that profited from renewed interest in the holiday. Other writers and publishers immediately devised ideas for the next season, and many new titles appeared in shops by the end of the following year. In the meantime, a few months after the book had become a vast success, Dickens rewarded Chapman and Hall's lack of faith in his idea by ending his contract with them and moving to a different publisher.

By the time he died in 1870, Dickens's name had become synonymous with the holiday. Overheard in Covent Garden Market,

"He dressed himself all in his best, and at last got out into the streets. The people were by this time pouring forth, as he had seen them with the Ghost of Christmas Present; and walking with his hands behind him, Scrooge regarded every one with a delighted smile. He looked so irresistibly pleasant, in a word, that three or four good-humoured fellows said, 'Good morning, sir. A merry Christmas to you.' And Scrooge said often afterwards, that of all the blithe sounds he had ever heard, those were the blithest in his ears. . . . He went to church, and walked about the streets, and watched the people hurrying to and fro, and patted children on the head, and questioned beggars, and looked down into the kitchens of houses, and up to the windows, and found that everything could yield him pleasure. He had never dreamed that any walk—that anything—could give him so much happiness."

—From *A Christmas Carol*
by Charles Dickens, 1843

a little girl asked, "If Mr. Dickens is dead, does that mean Father Christmas will die, too?"

OTHER CHRISTMAS NOVELLAS BY CHARLES DICKENS
After the success of *A Christmas Carol*, readers and, of course, his new publisher clamoured for more. At the time, Dickens was living with his family in Italy for a year. Influenced by the sound of bells ringing in Italian churches, Dickens wrote *The Chimes*, published in December 1844. Bradbury and Evans, his new publisher, released *The Cricket on the Hearth* in 1845 and, in 1846, *The Battle of Life*, written in Switzerland. Dickens disliked the constant pressure to focus on seasonal writing, so he skipped 1847, much to the public's disappointment. His fifth and final Christmas book, *The Haunted Man and the Ghost's Bargain*, appeared in 1848. It tells of a man grieving the death of his sister, echoing Dickens's own sadness at losing his much-loved older sister, Frances, who died of consumption that year. After *The Haunted Man*, Dickens pivoted to short stories for the Christmas market. In 1850, he founded *Household Words*, his first magazine, for which he commissioned other writers to create Christmas stories as well.

CHRISTMAS GHOST STORIES
A Christmas Carol unwittingly created a new subgenre of fiction: the Christmas ghost story.

Every year, *Household Words*—which Dickens replaced some years later with *All the Year Round*, his second magazine—published a special Christmas edition. Intended to be read aloud, many holiday stories commissioned for those issues—including "The Old Nurse's Story" by Elizabeth Gaskell (1852), "The Deaf Playmate's Story" by Harriet Martineau (1852), and Dickens's own "The Signalman" (1866)—contained ghosts or other unsettling aspects that

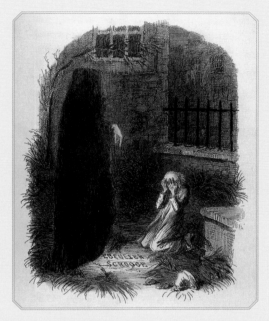

The Ghost of Christmas Yet to Come points to Ebenezer Scrooge's gravestone

made reading spooky tales an essential part of Christmas festivities into the 1900s. Other authors capitalised on the demand, creating works such as "The Ghost in the Clock Room" by Hesba Stretton (1859), "The Body Snatcher" by Robert Louis Stevenson (1884), "Christmas Eve on a Haunted Hulk" by Frank Cowper (1889), and "Lost Hearts" by M. R. James (1895).

"Grantræet" (The Fir-Tree) and "Snedronningen" (The Snow Queen) by Hans Christian Andersen, 1844

The first of these tales tells the story of a tree as it grows from a seed to full size. Never happy in the moment, it always eagerly awaits its next stage of life. It doesn't enjoy what it can see from its current height, constantly yearning to be taller. It longs to be cut down for use as ship timbers and becomes sad when other trees are chosen instead. When chopped down to serve as a Christmas tree, it thinks it will be happy, but it realises, too late, that it *was* happy in the forest and yearns to be back there. At the end of the story, the tree is chopped into firewood.

"The Snow Queen" begins with the tale of a hobgoblin who creates a mirror that magnifies everything bad and ugly and shrinks everything good or kind. The mirror smashes into millions of pieces. Later, two neighbouring children, Gerda and Kay, become friends and play together. During a snowstorm, Gerda's grandmother tells the children that snowflakes are "white bees that are swarming" and that the Snow Queen rules these snow bees. One summer's evening, Kay spots the Snow Queen and fears her. The following day, Kay feels sharp pain in his eye and heart, caused by two shards from the magic mirror. Kay changes and his friendship with Gerda sours. Sledging with other children, Kay meets the Snow Queen, who takes him away in her sleigh. When he doesn't return, everyone thinks him dead, but Gerda refuses to believe it. Through several countries, she searches for him until she finds the Snow Queen's palace and rescues him.

"The Christmas Banquet" by Nathaniel Hawthorne, 1846

Imagine a Christmas for which the ten most miserable people in town gather every year at a sombre banquet. That's the premise of this short story, in which the guests, seated with a skeleton, share their misery around the table.

The step of Time stole onward, and soon brought merry Christmas round again, with glad and solemn worship in the churches, and sports, games, festivals, and

everywhere the bright face of Joy beside the household
fire. Again likewise the hall, with its curtains of dusky
purple, was illuminated by the death-torches gleaming
on the sepulchral decorations of the banquet. The
veiled, skeleton sat in state, lifting the cypress-wreath
above its head, as the guerdon of some guest illustrious
in the qualifications which there claimed precedence.

Written in Salem, Massachusetts, Hawthorne's gothic, unseasonally
seasonal tale clearly owes a debt to his Puritan ancestors.

"Christmas Storms and Sunshine" by Elizabeth Gaskell, 1848

Howitt's Journal published this satirical yet warmhearted tale of
warring neighbours becoming friends. The remarkably modern first
paragraph details the political differences between the two newspapers for which the two husbands work: "the *Flying Post* was long
established and respectable—alias bigoted and Tory; the *Examiner*
was spirited and intelligent—alias new-fangled and democratic."
These differences spill into the men's lives, making them dislike
each other. At home, their wives also feud. Mrs. Hodgson has a
baby, of which the childless Mrs. Jenkins is jealous. Mrs. Jenkins
has a much-loved cat, which Mrs. Hodgson beats after it steals her
food. When the Hodgson baby becomes ill, Mrs. Jenkins helps save
his life. At the end of the story, the couples sit down to Christmas
dinner together.

Gaskell's first novel, *Mary Barton*—which exposed the appalling
working conditions of the labouring classes—also appeared in 1848,
albeit anonymously. Sensing a kindred spirit, Dickens sought her
out and became good friends with her and her husband. Dickens
frequently commissioned Mrs. Gaskell to write for him.

"The Christmas Shadrach"
by Frank Stockton, 1891

This sweet, witty short story begins with the narrator searching for a Christmas gift for Mildred, a friend since childhood who, he worries, is falling in love with him. He has fallen for Janet, a flirtatious young woman, so he seeks a gift for Mildred that will discourage her from thinking of him in a romantic way. In an antique shop, he spots a paperweight made from a purple mineral called Shadrach. The shop owner elaborates: "Some people think there is a sort of magical quality . . . that it can give out to human beings something of its power to keep their minds cool." The paperweight has the desired effect, but the narrator doesn't like the result. In a convoluted series of events, the paperweight changes hands several times until Mildred falls back in love with him, and the tale ends happily for all concerned.

"The Adventure of the Blue Carbuncle"
by Arthur Conan Doyle, 1892

Introduced in *A Study in Scarlet*, published in 1887, Sherlock Holmes and John Watson became an immediate hit with the reading public. Several years later, *The Strand* magazine published this seasonal story about the consulting detective and his medical companion that tells of a stolen jewel and a lost Christmas goose. In this extract, Holmes explains the start of the mystery to Watson.

> The facts are these: about four o'clock on Christmas morning, Peterson, who, as you know, is a very honest fellow, was returning from some small jollification and was making his way homeward down Tottenham Court Road. In front of him he saw, in the gaslight, a tallish man, walking with a slight stagger, and

carrying a white goose slung over his shoulder. As
he reached the corner of Goodge Street, a row broke
out between this stranger and a little knot of roughs.
One of the latter knocked off the man's hat, on which
he raised his stick to defend himself and, swinging it
over his head, smashed the shop window behind him.
Peterson had rushed forward to protect the stranger
from his assailants; but the man, shocked at having
broken the window, and seeing an official-looking
person in uniform rushing towards him, dropped
his goose, took to his heels, and vanished amid the
labyrinth of small streets which lie at the back of
Tottenham Court Road. The roughs had also fled
at the appearance of Peterson, so that he was left in
possession of the field of battle, and also of the spoils
of victory in the shape of this battered hat and a most
unimpeachable Christmas goose.

Preparing the goose to be cooked, Peterson discovered the stolen
jewel inside it. Then the real Christmas mystery begins.

The Christmas Hirelings
by Mary Braddon, 1894

Mary Braddon, prolific and renowned in her time, has faded from
popular memory, like too many women writers of the Victorian age.
This novel tells of a lonely old man who opens his manor to three working children for the holiday season. As Braddon wrote in the preface,
the inspiration for the story came to her while chatting with friends.

I had long wished to write a story about children,
which should be interesting to childish readers, and

"Children, yes, of course! Nobody knows how to enjoy Christmas if he has no children to make happy. If one has no children of one's own, one ought to hire some for the Christmas week—children to cram with mince pies and plum pudding; children to take to the pantomime; children to let off crackers; children to take on the ice. I have any number of godchildren scattered about among the houses of my friends, and I feel half a century younger when I am romping with them. What do you think of my notion, Miss Hawberk? Don't you think it would be a good dodge to hire some children for Christmas Day?"

—From *The Christmas Hirelings* by Mary Braddon, 1894

yet not without interest for grown-up people: but that desire might never have been realized without the unexpected impulse of a suggestion, dropped casually in the freedom of conversation at a table where the clever hostess is ever an incentive to bright thoughts. The talk was of Christmas; and almost everybody agreed that the season, considered from the old-fashioned festal standpoint, was pure irony. Was it not a time of extra burdens, of manifold claims upon everybody's purse and care, of great expectations from all sorts of people, of worry and weariness? Except for the children! There we were unanimous.

Christmas was the children's festival—for us a rush and a scramble, and a perpetual paying away of money; for them a glimpse of Fairyland.

"If we had no children of our own," said my left-hand neighbour, "we ought to hire some for Christmas."

CHRISTMAS GIFTS

"Whenever I make a Christmas present I like it to mean some-thing, not necessarily my sentiments toward the person to whom I give it, but sometimes an expression of what I should like that person to do or to be."
—From "The Christmas Shadrach" by Frank Stockton, 1891

In antiquity, even before the rise of Rome, people exchanged gifts to mark the new year. The ancient Romans continued the tradition, with the new year restoring order after the excesses of Saturnalia.

When Christianity became the official religion of the empire and, later, the rest of Europe, giving gifts at the start of the new year continued, echoing the biblical story of the Magi or Three Kings bringing gifts to the baby Jesus at Epiphany (the 6th of January). Over the centuries, different countries settled on varying gift-giving days, including the Feast of St. Nicholas (the 6th of December), Christmas Eve, Christmas Day, New Year's Day, and Epiphany (Three Kings Day or Twelfth Night).

The expression *Christmas present* first appeared in print in English in 1769. Throughout the 1800s, increasing numbers of European countries—and some of the countries they had colonised—adopted the practice of giving gifts either on the 24th or 25th of December. By the end of the century, gift-giving had become an accepted and expected part of holiday festivities.

BOARD GAMES

Many board games popular in Victorian times haven't survived, but some remain well known today, including checkers/draughts, chess, Pachisi/Sorry!/Ludo, and Chutes/Snakes and Ladders. They don't have a specifically Christmas connotation, but many people played them then to pass the time.

Maricourt: The Laughable Game of Courtship and Marriage, a nineteenth-century board game, called for teams of one man and one woman to advance their counters, through the pitfalls of courtship and betrothal to marriage. With each throw of the dice, the counter risked falling prey to jealousy, flirting (so scandalous that the square sent that team back to the beginning), disdain, affectation, contempt, despair, and other dating obstacles. Happier squares included affection, wealth, Papa's consent, and love. Landing on the final square, which depicted a church, won the game.

"Palace of Saint Nicholas in the Moon,
Christmas Morning

My Dear Susy Clemens,

   I have received and read all the letters which you
and your little sister have written me. . . . I can read
your and your baby sister's jagged and fantastic marks
without any trouble at all. But I had trouble with
those letters which you dictated through your mother
and the nurses, for I am a foreigner and cannot read
English writing well. You will find that I made no mis-
takes about the things which you and the baby ordered
in your own letters—I went down your chimney at
midnight when you were asleep and delivered them all
myself—and kissed both of you, too. . . . But . . . there
were . . . one or two small orders which I could not fill
because we ran out of stock."

—From "A Letter from Santa Claus"
by Mark Twain, 1875

Le Tour du Monde en Quatre-Vingts Jours (Around the World in Eighty Days) by Jules Verne, an adventure novel published in 1872, inspired American journalist Nellie Bly, the pen name of Elizabeth Cochrane, to undertake a similar challenge in real life in November 1889. She made it around the world in 72 days, a media feat that served as the title of her own book. Released in 1890, the Round the World with Nellie Bly board game followed her travels and adventures. Players competed to travel around the globe as fast as possible with the risk of landing on squares that could stall them.

WASSAILING

In agricultural communities, the ancient tradition of wassailing involved drinking a toast to fruit trees to encourage a bountiful harvest. The word comes from *ves heill*, an Old Norse salutation meaning "Be well!" The toast evolved into the first part of a call and response, with "drinkhail" as the reply. Around 1300, the definition of the word *wassail* shifted to designate the beverage used for the toast, usually called "punch" today. The concoction included a low-proof alcohol, such as ale, cider, or mead, combined with spices and fruit, such as apples and pears, sometimes with a crust of bread at the bottom. Wassail bowls came out not only for Christmas but also New Year's Eve and Twelfth Night.

A CHRISTMAS SWIM

On Christmas Day 1864, the Serpentine Swimming Club established an annual race in the Serpentine in Hyde Park, London. It has taken place every year except for 2020 (because of the Covid-19 lockdown). In the frigid lake water, participants compete to swim

100 metres. In harsh winters, they have to break the ice before they can enter. In the late 1800s, the winner received a medal. Christmas swims also take place in many other parts of the world.

MYSTERY PLAYS

Since the Middle Ages, many Christian countries have featured mystery or miracle plays at Easter, and similar performances once proved common at Christmastime as well. With low rates of literacy and education, these presentations helped reinforce religious stories and traditions in much the same way as stained glass and tapestries in churches depicted biblical scenes. Through these plays and images, those unable to read could experience the religious narratives.

MUMMING

From once-prevalent mystery plays grew the practice of mumming, the word deriving either from a German or Greek word for a disguise or mask. In English, the name for these usually male performers is mummers; in Scotland, guisards. From the local community but suitably disguised, mummers travel from house to house, performing Christmas-themed scenes. Traditional characters include St. George, Alexander the King of Egypt, Hector (or Slasher), a dragon, a doctor, Robin Redbreast (usually played by a little boy), and Father Christmas, who delivers the prologue and narrates the performances. In aristocratic households, the tradition entailed elaborate theatrical performances. As with many old, rural traditions, mumming became less prevalent with the Industrial Revolution, when many people moved from the countryside to cities.

Three mummers, from *The Navy & Army Illustrated*, 1899

PANTOMIME

"Hurrah for the Pantomime! It has been truly said, that as well might the festive season find its way upon us round the annual calendar, without its snowy mantle, than that we should welcome Christmas without a pantomime."
—From *The Pantomimes and All about Them* by Leopold Wagner, 1881

In eighteenth-century London, a new form of theatre entranced audiences. Pantomime, now an iconic form of British Christmas fun, began as an offshoot of commedia dell'arte, an Italian entertainment. The earliest pantomimes adapted classic stories from literature and mythology but soon evolved into high-energy, slapstick performances lampooning contemporary society and politics.

By the middle of the 1800s, pantomime had become an outlandish riot of characters with huge personalities, elaborate costumes, and a great deal of audience participation. Victorian audiences, consisting largely of children, took in performances based on folklore and fairy tales, including "Dick Whittington," "Jack and the Beanstalk," and "Cinderella." During the Victorian age, the art form attained many of its quintessential features: the pantomime dame played by a male actor in women's clothing; the principal boy played by a woman in men's clothing; and a clown figure. Pantomime reflects current society, so the scripts feature references and jokes about current events, celebrities, and politicians. As a child, Dickens enjoyed watching the great clown Grimaldi perform in pantomime. By the end of the century, pantomime didn't always include an actual clown, with a comic figure fulfilling the role instead.

The Waits

Washington Irving mentions the Waits in *The Sketch Book of Geoffrey Crayon,* published in 1819.

> I had scarcely got into bed when a strain of music seemed to break forth in the air just below the window. I listened, and found it proceeded from a band which I concluded to be the Waits from some neighbouring village. They went round the house, playing under the windows. . . . The sounds, as they receded, became more soft and aerial, and seemed to accord with the quiet and moonlight. I listened and listened—they became more and more tender and remote, and, as they gradually died away, my head sunk upon the pillow and I fell asleep.

Dickens also wrote about the phenomenon in "The Seven Poor Travellers," a short story published in 1854.

> As I passed along the High Street, I heard the Waits at a distance, and struck off to find them. They were playing near one of the old gates of the City, at the corner of a wonderfully quaint row of red-brick tenements, which the clarionet obligingly informed me were inhabited by the Minor-Canons. . . . The clarionet was so communicative, and my inclinations were (as they generally are) of so vagabond a tendency, that I accompanied the Waits across an open green called the Vines, and assisted—in the French sense—at the

ACTIVITIES

performance of two waltzes, two polkas, and three
Irish melodies, before I thought of my inn any more.

At the end of the century, Thomas Crippen, a cleric, librarian, and
hymnologist, began compiling a history of holiday customs and folklore. Four decades of research resulted in *Christmas and Christmas
Lore*, published in 1923. In it, he notes that "By the beginning of
the eighteenth century these [the Town Watchmen] had, in some
places, become the Town Musicians, to whom the term 'the Waits'
is applied in *The Tatler*. . . . On the whole, the word seems most nat-
urally to refer to watching and waiting, and may remind us that of
old Christmas began in the evening."

No one has provided a fully satisfactory etymology for the term.
It may come from Old English *wayte*, a musical instrument like an
oboe. In a time before organised police forces, it also could refer to
watchmen waiting for something to happen. As Crippen notes, many
watchmen played musical instruments while on patrol, perhaps to
reassure the townspeople of their presence.

ROUND THE WORLD
WITH
NELLIE BLY.

A NOVEL AND FASCINATING GAME WITH PLENTY
OF EXCITEMENT ON LAND AND SEA.

M? LOUGHLIN BROS., NEW YORK.

CHRISTMAS ACTIVITIES

Christmas Cards

This Victorian tradition still holds strong, so you don't need instructions for how to do it. Consider taking a page from the earliest days of the era, though, and write longhand letters to loved ones, with pen on paper. With apologies to Henry Cole, a handwritten letter means so much more than a store-bought card.

In whatever you send, don't be afraid to use the very old word *Xmas*. As Charles Dodgson, a famous Victorian better known by the pen name Lewis Carroll, wrote to a friend in 1890: "*One* piece of work, at any rate, I am clear ought to be done this year, and it will take months of hard work: I mean the second volume of 'Sylvie and Bruno.' I fully *mean*, if I have life and health till Xmas next, to bring it out then."

Christmas Stories

This book doesn't have room to reprint all the Victorian Christmas stories worth investigating, ghostly or otherwise, so here's a select reading list of works that appeared during Queen Victoria's lifetime (1819–1901). Note that, per tradition, not all the ghostly stories mention or touch on Christmas. To experience them in the Victorian way, read sections or chapters aloud, taking turns with loved ones. For even more fun, do a group reading by assigning the roles of narrator and speaking characters to different members of your group.

> "Christmas" by Washington Irving, 1820
> "The Stage Coach" by Washington Irving, 1820
> "Christmas Eve" by Washington Irving, 1820
> "Christmas Day" by Washington Irving, 1820
> "The Christmas Dinner" by Washington Irving, 1820

The Keeping of Christmas at Bracebridge Hall
    by Washington Irving, 1822
"Account of a Visit from St. Nicholas,"
    by Clement Moore, 1823
"The Tapestried Chamber" by Walter Scott, 1828
"The Night Before Christmas" by Nikolai Gogol, 1832
"Christmas Festivities" by Charles Dickens, 1835
A Christmas Carol by Charles Dickens, 1843
"The Fir-Tree" by Hans Christian Andersen, 1844
"The Snow Queen" by Hans Christian Andersen, 1844
The Chimes by Charles Dickens, 1844
The Nutcracker by Alexandre Dumas, 1844
The Cricket on the Hearth by Charles Dickens, 1845
The Battle of Life by Charles Dickens, 1846
"The Christmas Banquet" by Nathaniel Hawthorne, 1846
The Haunted Man and the Ghost's Bargain
    by Charles Dickens, 1848
"Christmas Storms and Sunshine" by Elizabeth Gaskell, 1848
"A Christmas Tree" by Charles Dickens, 1850
"What Christmas Is, As We Grow Older"
    by Charles Dickens, 1851
"The Old Nurse's Story" by Elizabeth Gaskell, 1852
"The Deaf Playmate's Story" by Harriet Martineau, 1852
"A Mysterious Visitor" by Ellen Wood, 1857
"The Ghost in the Clock Room" by Hesba Stretton, 1859
"Horror: A True Tale" by John Berwick Harwood, 1861
"Bring Me a Light!" by Jane Hooper, 1861
"Old Hooker's Ghost," 1865
"The Signalman" by Charles Dickens, 1866
"The Ghost's Summons" by Ada Buisson, 1868
"Jack Layford's Friend" by L. N., 1869

"How Peter Parley Laid a Ghost," 1875

The Lady's Walk by Margaret Oliphant (novel), 1882

"The Lady's Walk" by Margaret Oliphant (short story) 1883

"The Captain of the Pole-Star" by Arthur Conan Doyle, 1883

"The Body Snatcher" by Robert Louis Stevenson, 1884

"The Haunted Rock" by W. W. Fenn, 1885

"The Canterville Ghost" by Oscar Wilde, 1887

"Christmas Eve on a Haunted Hulk" by Frank Cowper, 1889

"The Christmas Shadrach" by Frank Stockton, 1891

"The Adventure of the Blue Carbuncle"
    by Arthur Conan Doyle, 1892

The Christmas Hirelings by Mary Braddon, 1894

"Lost Hearts" by M. R. James, 1895

The Doll's Ghost by F. Marion Crawford, 1896

GAMES

In an age before radio, cinema, television, video games, the Internet, and other diversions, Victorians made their own amusements. Music formed a big part of their social life, and most gatherings involved guests listening to it, singing, dancing, or some combination of the three. These board games and parlour games also proved popular.

Board Games

Spend some quality time with family or friends in true Victorian Christmas style, playing one or more of the following board games.

Balderdash: This board game translates the Dictionary Game or Fictionary, a parlour game, onto a flat surface.

Checkers/draughts.

Chess.

The board from Round the World with Nellie Bly

Chutes/Snakes and Ladders: Originating in ancient India, this game came to Britain in the 1890s.

The Game of Life: Created by Milton Bradley in 1860, this game, sometimes called just Life, makes a friendly competition of making it from infancy, through college, marriage, and children, to retirement.

Pachisi: This game and its name brand variations—Parcheesi, Sorry!, and Ludo, all played on a board in the shape of a symmetrical cross—also originated in ancient India. In Hindi, *paccīs* means "twenty-five," the largest score possible in the original.

Parlour Games
"The office was closed in a twinkling, and the clerk, with the long ends of his white comforter dangling below his waist (for he boasted no great-coat), went down a slide on Cornhill, at the end

of a lane of boys, twenty times, in honour of its being Christmas Eve, and then ran home to Camden Town as hard as he could pelt, to play at blindman's-buff."
—From *A Christmas Carol* by Charles Dickens, 1843

BLIND MAN'S BUFF

From a group of people, one person wears a blindfold. Held by the shoulders and spun around several times, that person must try to catch someone while everyone tries to evade capture. If the blind-folded person touches someone else, the captured person stops moving. The blindfold then goes onto the person captured, and the game resumes.

CHARADES

From literary charades, a riddle game popular in France in the 1700s, came the practice of silently acting charades, the game as we know it today. It appears in *Jane Eyre* by Charlotte Brontë, *Vanity Fair* by William Thackeray, and other Victorian novels.

Divide players into two groups of equal number. Each group receives a pen, the same number of slips of paper, and a bowl. On each slip of paper, players write a word or phrase, such as a play or book title (for the purposes of this book, preferably Victorian!). Fold the slips and place them in the bowl. The teams then swap bowls. Before you begin, decide how much time each charade can run (for example, one, two, or five minutes).

A player from Team 1 takes a slip of paper from the Team 2 bowl, ensuring that no one on Team 1 can see the word or phrase. In the middle of the room, the player acts out the word or phrase, without speaking or making other noises. The player's teammates must guess the word or phrase before time runs out. A correct guess gains one point. If time runs out, no point is awarded. After the first go, a player from Team 2 follows the same ritual, and the game continues until the players have acted out all the slips of paper. The team with the most points wins.

I LOVE MY LOVE

In this word game, each player says, "I love my love because—" and adds an appropriate phrase. Player 1 must choose a word beginning with "A," and players must cycle through the alphabet in turn.

Player 1: "I love my love because she is *adorable*."

Player 2: "I love my love because he is *brilliant*."

Player 3: "I love my love because she is *clever*."

At the end of the alphabet, players can start again, this time finding *two* words that begin with the same letter. They don't have to flatter; they just have to fit the pattern!

Player 1: "I love my love because she is *xenophobic* and plays the *xylophone*."

Player 2: "I love my love because he is *youthful* and a *yodeller*."

Player 3: "I love my love because she is *zany* and *zesty*."

The game can continue for as long as players can cope. For example, round 3 could start like this:

Player 1: "I love my love because he is *active* and *affable* and grows *apricots*."

Player 2: "I love my love because she is *beautiful* and *brainy* and plays *ball*."

Player 3: "I love my love because he is *cantankerous* and *caustic* and likes *cheese*."

THE PARSON'S CAT

In this word game that also improves vocabulary, players go through the letters of the alphabet in order. Each player follows the formula, proceeding to the next letter of the alphabet as they play.

Player 1: "The parson's cat is an *adventurous* cat. He lives in *Africa* and eats *apples*."

Player 2: "The parson's cat is a *blissful* cat. She lives in *Boston* and eats *burgers*."

Player 3: "The parson's cat is a *creative* cat. He lives in *Copenhagen* and eats *cotton_candy*."

The game continues until reaching the letter *z*. To play a second round, players must avoid using the same words chosen by the previous person who had that letter.

PASS THE THIMBLE

Players form a circle, facing inward, and one person stands in the middle. One person in the circle has a thimble or small object that fits in the palm, such as a marble or die. The person in the middle closes his or her eyes. As silently as possible, the players in the circle pass the thimble around. At any moment, the player in the middle can open his or her eyes and guess who's holding the thimble. If the guess is correct, the person holding the thimble moves into the middle, the person who guessed correctly joins the circle, and the game begins again.

SNAPDRAGON

This dangerous game appears purely for historical reference. Don't attempt it! Victorians covered a plate with raisins and nuts, dousing them with brandy. In a dark room, they placed the plate on a table and set the brandy alight. Players reached into the flames to pluck as

Snapdragon by Edmund Garrett, 1889

many of the fruits and nuts as they could grab. In the 1800s, the game proved so popular that Lewis Carroll joked about it in *Through the Looking-Glass, and What Alice Found There* by turning the game into a creature: " 'Look on the branch above your head,' said the Gnat, 'and there you'll find a snap-dragon-fly. Its body is made of plum-pudding, its wings of holly-leaves, and its head is a raisin burning in brandy.'

'And what does it live on?'

'Frumenty and mince pie,' the Gnat replied; 'and it makes its nest in a Christmas box.' "

SQUEAK, PIGGY, SQUEAK

One player plays the farmer, blindfolded and holding a cushion, while everyone else plays a piggy. The piggies place chairs in a circle around the farmer. One of them spins the farmer around, who must wait for all the piggies to sit in the chairs. The farmer finds his or her way to the piggies and, upon finding one in a chair, sets the cushion on the person's lap, taking care not to touch the person. Sitting on the cushion, the farmer then says "Squeak, piggy, squeak!" and the piggy must squeak. The farmer must guess the piggy's identity from the squeak alone. If the farmer is correct, the piggy becomes the farmer. If the farmer says the wrong name, someone spins the farmer around, and the game begins again.

YES AND NO

In this game, similar to Twenty Questions, a chosen player stands in the middle of the room and assumes the identity of someone else, famous or otherwise known to the group, answering questions from the group, such as "Are you a child?" "Are you from Australia?" "Are you female?" "Are you an athlete?" "Do you write books?" and so on.

The player in the middle can answer only "yes" or "no," so questions must be phrased carefully. An accidental either/or question—"Are you from Mexico or New York?"—cannot be answered. The person who correctly guesses the character's identity wins. The winner moves to the middle of the room, and the game begins again.

WASSAILING

By definition, wassailing involves drinking alcohol and singing carols (page 141) door to door, not always an advisable combination! Rather than risking intoxication in public, save the quaffing for *after* the singing, as a reward for songs well sung.

Wassailing the apples

A Christmas Swim

You don't have to live near Hyde Park in London or even in Britain to participate in a Victorian Christmas swim. If you live near an appropriate body of water, (safely) jump in! Bring a change of clothes and don't stay in too long—unless you live in the Southern Hemisphere, where a Christmas swim on a hot day can cool you down.

Seasonal Performances

Mystery plays may prove hard to find, though many churches produce nativity plays for Christmas. In Britain, you should be able to find local mumming or pantomime events without too much difficulty. In America, the easiest Victorian performance to attend will be *The Nutcracker* ballet, composed by Pyotr Tchaikovsky in 1892.

Carols

"Before I go, just let me say one thing.

If any of you have any quarrels, or misunderstandings, or coolnesses, or cold shoulders, or shynesses, or tiffs, or miffs, or huffs, with any one else, just make friends before Christmas,—you will be so much merrier if you do.

I ask it of you for the sake of that old angelic song, heard so many years ago by the shepherds, keeping watch by night, on Bethlehem Heights."

**—From "Christmas Storms and Sunshine"
by Elizabeth Gaskell, 1848**

HE WORD *carol* originally meant a dance that involved singing. By the early 1300s, the meaning had shifted to denote songs sung at major Christian festivals. Eventually, those songs focused just on Christmas, then fell from fashion during the Protestant Reformation and the English and Scottish Commonwealth. By the late 1700s, the Christmas carol had returned to favour, and *Christmas Carols, Ancient and Modern* by William Sandys, published in 1833, further energised their revival. They gained continued popularity throughout the century. After the death of Queen Victoria in 1901, composer and musicologist Cecil Sharp began a campaign to collect, document, and save English folk songs and music, which included a number of Christmas carols.

"Fine old Christmas, with the snowy hair and ruddy face, had done his duty that year in the noblest fashion, and had set off his rich gifts of warmth and colour with all the heightening contrast of frost and snow. . . . There had been singing under the windows after midnight,—supernatural singing, Maggie always felt, in spite of Tom's contemptuous insistence that the singers were old Patch, the parish clerk, and the rest of the church choir; she trembled with awe when their carolling broke in upon her dreams, and the image of men in fustian clothes was always thrust away by the vision of angels resting on the parted cloud."

—From *The Mill on the Floss*
by George Eliot, 1860

CHRISTMAS CAROLS

The First Nowell

History doesn't record the name of the author of this carol. The song likely originated in Cornwall in the 1200s. In 1823, Davies Gilbert included it in *Some Ancient Christmas Carols*. A spelling variant, *Noël* means "Christmas" in French.

The first Nowell the angel did say
was to certain poor shepherds in fields as they lay,
in fields where they lay keeping their sheep,
on a cold winter's night that was so deep.
Nowell, Nowell, Nowell, Nowell,
born is the King of Israel.

They looked up and saw a star
shining in the east beyond them far;
and to the earth it gave great light,
and so it continued both day and night.
Nowell, Nowell, Nowell, Nowell,
born is the King of Israel.

And by the light of that same star,
three wise men came from country far;
to seek for a king was their intent,
and to follow the star wherever it went.
Nowell, Nowell, Nowell, Nowell,
born is the King of Israel.

This star drew nigh to the northwest;
o'er Bethlehem it took its rest,
   and there it did both stop and stay,
   right over the place where Jesus lay.
Nowell, Nowell, Nowell, Nowell,
born is the King of Israel.

Then entered in those wise men three,
full reverently upon their knee,
   and offered there in his presence
   their gold, and myrrh, and frankincense.
Nowell, Nowell, Nowell, Nowell,
born is the King of Israel.

Then let us all with one accord
sing praises to our heavenly Lord,
   that hath made heaven and earth of nought,
   and with his blood our life hath bought.
Nowell, Nowell, Nowell, Nowell,
born is the King of Israel.

O Christmas Tree

In 1824, Ernst Anschütz, a German composer, adapted and extended "Ach Tannenbaum," an old Polish folk song by Melchior Franck, into this carol. A *tannenbaum* is just a fir tree, not specifically a Christmas tree, but firs often serve as Christmas trees, so the association followed.

O Christmas tree, O Christmas tree,
how faithful are your branches,
   not only green when summer's here
   but in the coldest time of year.
O Christmas tree, O Christmas tree,
how faithful are your branches!

O Christmas tree, O Christmas tree,
much pleasure do you bring me!
   For every year the Christmas tree
   brings to us all both joy and glee.
O Christmas tree, O Christmas tree,
much pleasure do you bring me!

O Christmas tree, O Christmas tree,
your raiment holds a lesson:
   that hope and durance in all climes
   give strength and courage at all times!
O Christmas tree, O Christmas tree,
your raiment holds a lesson!

I Saw Three Ships

Definitive origins for this song remain obscure. The earliest version comes from the 1600s, likely in Derbyshire. This version comes from *Christmastide: Its History, Festivities, and Carols* by antiquarian William Sandys, published in 1833, which increased the song's popularity through the rest of the century.

I saw three ships come sailing in
on Christmas Day, on Christmas Day;
I saw three ships come sailing in
on Christmas Day in the morning.

And who was in those ships all three
on Christmas Day, on Christmas Day?
And who was in those ships all three,
on Christmas Day in the morning?

Our Saviour Christ and his ladye
on Christmas Day, on Christmas Day;
Our Saviour Christ and his ladye,
on Christmas Day in the morning.

Pray whither sailed those ships all three
on Christmas Day, on Christmas Day?
Pray whither sailed those ships all three,
on Christmas Day in the morning?

continues 🎄

O they sailed into Bethlehem
on Christmas Day, on Christmas Day;
O they sailed into Bethlehem,
on Christmas Day in the morning.

And all the bells on Earth shall ring
on Christmas Day, on Christmas Day;
And all the bells on Earth shall ring
on Christmas Day in the morning.

And all the angels in Heaven shall sing
on Christmas Day, on Christmas Day;
And all the angels in Heaven shall sing
on Christmas Day in the morning.

And all the souls on Earth shall sing
on Christmas Day, on Christmas Day;
and all the souls on Earth shall sing
on Christmas Day in the morning.

SILENT NIGHT

Austrian priest Josephus Mohr penned the lyrics to "Stille Nacht" ("Silent Night") in 1816, to which his friend Franz Gruber later set the accompanying music. The carol was first performed in 1818 and first published in 1833, and its fame spread far and wide. It has appeared in more than 300 languages, and UNESCO has designated it a piece of intangible cultural heritage.

Silent night! Holy night!
All is calm, all is bright
   'round yon virgin mother and child.
   Holy infant, so tender and mild,
sleep in heavenly peace,
sleep in heavenly peace.

Silent night! Holy night!
Shepherds quake at the sight!
   Glories stream from heaven afar,
   heav'nly hosts sing alleluia;
Christ, the Saviour, is born!
Christ, the Saviour, is born!

Silent night! Holy night!
Son of God, love's pure light,
   radiant beams from Thy holy face,
   with the dawn of redeeming grace,
Jesus, Lord, at Thy birth,
Jesus, Lord, at Thy birth.

Music on Christmas Morning

Writing as Acton Bell, Anne Brontë penned this poem, which appeared in print in 1846. Performed as a carol, it goes to the tune of "Pater Omnium."

Music I love—but never strain
   could kindle raptures so divine,
so grief assuage, so conquer pain,
   and rouse this pensive heart of mine—
     as that we hear on Christmas morn,
     upon the wintry breezes borne.

Though Darkness still her empire keep,
   and hours must pass ere morning break;
from troubled dreams or slumbers deep,
   that music kindly bids us wake:
     It calls us, with an angel's voice,
     to wake and worship and rejoice;

To greet with joy the glorious morn,
   which angels welcomed long ago,
when our redeeming Lord was born,
   to bring the light of Heaven below;
     the powers of Darkness to dispel,
     and rescue Earth from Death and Hell.

While listening to that sacred strain,
  my raptured spirit soars on high;
I seem to hear those songs again
  resounding through the open sky,
    that kindled such divine delight,
      in those who watched their flocks by night.

With them, I celebrate His birth—
  glory to God, in highest Heaven,
good-will to men and peace on earth,
  to us a Saviour-King is given;
    our God is come to claim His own,
      and Satan's power is overthrown!

A sinless God, for sinful men,
  descends to suffer and to bleed;
Hell must renounce its empire then;
  the price is paid, the world is freed,
    and Satan's self must now confess
      that Christ has earned a Right to bless:

Now holy Peace may smile from heaven,
  and heavenly Truth from earth shall spring:
The captive's galling bonds are riven,
  for our Redeemer is our king;
    and He that gave his blood for men
      will lead us home to God again.

The Holly and the Ivy

The spikes on holly leaves represent the crown of thorns, and the plant's red berries symbolise the shedding of Jesus's blood. Ivy long has served as a symbol for the Virgin Mary. Shorter versions of this carol appear in the early 1800s, but the full text comes from a book review published in 1849.

The holly and the ivy,
   when they are both full grown,
of all the trees that are in the wood,
   the holly bears the crown.
The rising of the sun
   and the running of the deer,
the playing of the merry organ,
   sweet singing in the choir.

The holly bears a blossom
   as white as the lily flower,
and Mary bore sweet Jesus Christ,
   to be our sweet Saviour.
The rising of the sun
   and the running of the deer,
the playing of the merry organ,
   sweet singing in the choir.

The holly bears a berry
   as red as any blood,
and Mary bore sweet Jesus Christ
   for to do us sinners good.

The rising of the sun
  and the running of the deer,
the playing of the merry organ,
  sweet singing in the choir.

The holly bears a prickle
  as sharp as any thorn,
and Mary bore sweet Jesus Christ
  on Christmas Day in the morn.
The rising of the sun
  and the running of the deer,
the playing of the merry organ,
  sweet singing in the choir.

The holly bears a bark
  as bitter as any gall,
and Mary bore sweet Jesus Christ
  for to redeem us all.
The rising of the sun
  and the running of the deer,
the playing of the merry organ,
  sweet singing in the choir.

The holly and the ivy,
  when they are both full grown,
of all the trees that are in the wood,
  the holly bears the crown.
The rising of the sun
  and the running of the deer,
the playing of the merry organ,
  sweet singing in the choir.

It Came upon the Midnight Clear

Written by Unitarian pastor Edmund Sears in 1849, the lyrics for this song first appeared as a poem published in the *Christian Register* in Boston. The next year, Richard Storrs Willis composed "Carol," the tune for it.

It came upon the midnight clear,
  that glorious song of old,
from angels bending near the earth
  to touch their harps of gold;
"Peace on the earth, good will to men
  from heaven's all-gracious King"—
The world in solemn stillness lay
  to hear the angels sing.

Still through the cloven skies they come,
  with peaceful wings unfurled,
and still their heavenly music floats
  o'er all the weary world;
above its sad and lowly plains,
  they bend on hovering wing,
and ever o'er its Babel sounds
  the blessed angels sing.

But with the woes of sin and strife
  the world has suffered long;
beneath the angel-strain have rolled
  Two-thousand years of wrong;

and man, at war with man, hears not
    the love-song which they bring;—
oh hush the noise, ye men of strife,
    and hear the angels sing!

And ye, beneath life's crushing load,
    whose forms are bending low,
who toil along the climbing way
    with painful steps and slow,
look now! For glad and golden hours
    come swiftly on the wing;—
oh, rest beside the weary road
    and hear the angels sing!

For lo! the days are hastening on,
    by prophet bards foretold,
when with the ever-circling years
    comes round the age of gold;
when peace shall over all the earth
    its ancient splendours fling,
and the whole world give back the song
    which now the angels sing.

Good King Wenceslas

For this song, John Mason Neale adapted a Czech poem by Václav Svoboda about St. Wenceslaus I, a duke of Bohemia posthumously made king. Thomas Helmore set it to "Tempus Adest Floridum" ("Eastertime Has Come"), a springtime carol from the 1200s.

Good King Wences'las looked out
　on the Feast of Stephen,
when the snow lay round about,
　deep and crisp and even;
brightly shone the moon that night,
　tho' the frost was cruel,
when a poor man came in sight,
　gath'ring winter fuel.

"Hither, page, and stand by me,
　if thou know'st it, telling,
yonder peasant, who is he?
　Where and what his dwelling?"
"Sire, he lives a good league hence,
　underneath the mountain;
right against the forest fence,
　by Saint Agnes' fountain."

"Bring me flesh, and bring me wine,
　bring me pine logs hither:
Thou and I shall see him dine
　when we bear them thither."

Page and monarch, forth they went,
    forth they went together;
through the rude wind's wild lament
    and the bitter weather.

"Sire, the night is darker now,
    and the wind blows stronger;
fails my heart, I know not how;
    I can go no longer."
"Mark my footsteps, my good page.
    Tread thou in them boldly.
Thou shalt find the winter's rage
    freeze thy blood less coldly."

In his master's steps he trod,
    where the snow lay dinted;
heat was in the very sod
    which the saint had printed.
Therefore, Christian men, be sure,
    wealth or rank possessing,
ye who now will bless the poor,
    shall yourselves find blessing.

O HOLY NIGHT

To commemorate the renovation of a church organ, French poet
Placide Cappeau wrote "Cantique de Noël," the original version of
these lyrics, in 1843, which Adolphe Adam set to music. In 1855,
John Dwight translated it into English.

> O holy night, the stars are brightly shining.
>   It is the night of the dear Saviour's birth.
> Long lay the world in sin and error pining
>   till He appeared and the soul felt its worth.
>
> A thrill of hope, the weary world rejoices,
>   for yonder breaks a new and glorious morn.
> Fall on your knees. O hear the angel voices,
>   O night divine, O night when Christ was born.
>
> Led by the light of faith serenely beaming,
>   with glowing hearts, by His cradle we stand.
> So led by light of a star sweetly gleaming,
>   here came the wise men from the orient land.
>
> The King of kings lay thus in lowly manger,
>   in all our trials born to be our friend.
> He knows our need, to our weakness no stranger.
>   Behold your King. Before Him lowly bend.

Truly He taught us to love one another.
 His law is love, and His gospel is peace.
Chains shall He break, for the slave is our brother,
 and in His name all oppression shall cease.

Sweet hymns of joy in grateful chorus raise we.
 Let all within us praise His holy name.
Christ is the Lord, then ever, ever praise we
 His power and glory evermore proclaim.

THE ONE-HORSE OPEN SLEIGH

James Lord Pierpont, uncle of financier John Pierpont Morgan,
wrote this song in a Massachusetts tavern. Published in 1857, it now
goes by the title "Jingle Bells." It doesn't mention Christmas, but
the association followed. The original lyrics appear below.

Dashing thro' the snow
in a one-horse open sleigh,
o'er the fields we go,
laughing all the way;
bells on bob tail ring,
making spirits bright.
What fun it is to ride and sing
a sleighing song tonight.

Jingle bells, jingle bells
jingle all the way;
Oh! what fun it is to ride
in a one-horse open sleigh.

A day or two ago,
I tho't I'd take a ride,
and soon Miss Fannie Bright
was seated by my side.
The horse was lean and lank.
Misfortune seemed his lot.
He got into a drifted bank,
and then we got upsot.

Jingle bells, jingle bells
   jingle all the way;
Oh! what fun it is to ride
   in a one-horse open sleigh.

A day or two ago,
   The story I must tell—
I went out on the snow,
   and on my back I fell;
A gent was riding by
   in a one-horse open sleigh;
He laughed, as there I sprawling lie,
   but quickly drove away.

Jingle bells, jingle bells
   jingle all the way;
Oh! what fun it is to ride
   in a one-horse open sleigh.

Now the ground is white.
   Go it while you're young;
take the girls tonight
   and sing this sleighing song;
just get a bobtailed bay,
   two-forty as his speed.
Hitch him to an open sleigh,
   and *crack!* you'll take the lead.

Jingle bells, jingle bells
   jingle all the way;
Oh! what fun it is to ride
   in a one-horse open sleigh.

THREE KINGS OF ORIENT

John Henry Hopkins Jr., rector of an Episcopal church in Pennsylvania, composed this carol in 1857 for a holiday procession in New York City.

[all]   We three kings of Orient are;
bearing gifts, we traverse afar,
field and fountain,
moor and mountain,
following yonder Star.

O star of wonder, star of night,
star with royal beauty bright,
westward leading,
still proceeding,
guide us to thy perfect light.

[Gaspard]   Born a king on Bethlehem plain,
gold I bring to crown Him again
King for ever,
ceasing never,
over us all to reign.

O star of wonder, star of night,
star with royal beauty bright,
westward leading,
still proceeding,
guide us to thy perfect light.

[Melchior]   Frankincense to offer have I;
incense owns a deity nigh:
  prayer and praising
  all men raising.
Worship Him God on high.

O star of wonder, star of night,
star with royal beauty bright,
  westward leading,
  still proceeding,
guide us to thy perfect light.

[Balthazar]   Myrrh is mine; its bitter perfume
breathes a life of gathering gloom;—
  sorrowing, sighing,
  bleeding, dying,
sealed in the stone-cold tomb.

O star of wonder, star of night,
star with royal beauty bright,
  westward leading,
  still proceeding,
guide us to thy perfect light.

[all]   Glorious now, behold Him arise,
King and God and sacrifice;
  Heav'n sings hallelujah:
  Hallelujah the earth replies.

continues ⟞

O star of wonder, star of night,
star with royal beauty bright,
　westward leading,
　still proceeding,
guide us to thy perfect light.

As with Gladness Men of Old

While ill in bed and unable to attend Epiphany services in 1859, William Dix wrote this poem, published a year later. For the music, added in 1861, William Monk adapted a tune by Conrad Kocher from 1838.

As with gladness men of old
did the guiding star behold;
    as with joy they hailed its light
    leading onward, beaming bright;
        so, most gracious God, may we
        evermore be led to Thee.

As with joyful steps they sped
to that lowly manger bed
    there to bend the knee before
    Thee, whom heaven and earth adore,
        so may we with willing feet
        ever seek Thy mercy-seat.

As they offered gifts most rare
at that manger rude and bare,
    so may we with holy joy,
    pure and free from sin's alloy
        all our costliest treasures bring,
        Christ, to Thee, our heavenly King.

continues

Holy Jesus, every day
keep us in the narrow way
  and, when earthly things are past,
  bring our ransomed souls at last
    where they need no star to guide,
    where no clouds Thy glory hide.

In the heavenly country bright,
need they no created light;
  Thou its light, its joy, its crown,
  Thou its sun, which goes not down.
    There forever may we sing
    Hallelujahs to our King.

Angels We Have Heard on High

This carol originated with a French song, "Les Anges dans Nos Campagnes" ("Angels in Our Countryside"), possibly by Wilfrid Moreau. Edward Shippen Barnes adapted the music, known as "Gloria," and James Chadwick, bishop of Hexham and Newcastle, adapted the lyrics into English, published in 1862.

Angels we have heard on high
  sweetly singing o'er the plains
and the mountains in reply,
  echoing their joyous strains.

Gloria in excelsis Deo!

Shepherds, why this jubilee?
  Why your joyous strains prolong?
What the gladsome tidings be?
  Which inspire your heavenly songs?

Gloria in excelsis Deo!

Come to Bethlehem and see
  Him Whose birth the angels sing;
Come, adore on bended knee,
  Christ the Lord, the newborn King.

Gloria in excelsis Deo!

See Him in a manger laid,
  Whom the choirs of angels praise;
Mary, Joseph, lend your aid,
  while our heart in love we raise.

Gloria in excelsis Deo!

DECK THE HALL

The melody of this song comes from "Nos Galan" ("New Year's Eve"), a Welsh song dating to the 1500s. Thomas Oliphant, a Scot, penned the English words in 1862. The original lyrics appear below.

Deck the hall with boughs of holly,
  fa, la, la, la, la, la, la, la, la!
'Tis the season to be jolly:
  fa, la, la, la, la, la, la, la, la!
Fill the meadcup, drain the barrel,
  fa, la, la, la, la, la, la, la, la!
Troul the ancient Christmas carol,
  fa, la, la, la, la, la, la, la, la!

See the flowing bowl before us,
  fa, la, la, la, la, la, la, la, la!
Strike the harp and join in chorus:
  fa, la, la, la, la, la, la, la, la!
Follow me in merry measure,
  fa, la, la, la, la, la, la, la, la!
while I sing of beauty's treasure,
  fa, la, la, la, la, la, la, la, la!

Fast away the old year passes,
  fa, la, la, la, la, la, la, la, la!
Hail the new, ye lads and lasses:
  fa, la, la, la, la, la, la, la, la!
laughing quaffing all together,
  fa, la, la, la, la, la, la, la, la!
heedless of the wind and weather,
  fa, la, la, la, la, la, la, la, la!

WHAT CHILD IS THIS?

In 1865, William Dix wrote the lyrics to this song and set it, several years later, to the traditional tune of "Greensleeves."

What Child is this Who, laid to rest,
on Mary's lap is sleeping?
Whom angels greet with anthems sweet
while shepherds watch are keeping?
This, this is Christ the King;
Whom shepherds guard and angels sing:
Haste, haste to bring Him laud,
the Babe, the Son of Mary.

Why lies He in such mean estate,
where ox and ass are feeding?
Good Christian, fear, for sinners here
the silent Word is pleading.
Nails, spear shall pierce Him through,
the cross be borne for me, for you:
Hail, hail, the Word made flesh,
the Babe, the Son of Mary!

So bring Him incense, gold, and myrrh.
Come peasant, king, to own Him:
The King of kings salvation brings.
Let loving hearts enthrone Him.
Raise, raise the song on high.
The Virgin sings her lullaby:
Joy, joy for Christ is born,
the Babe, the Son of Mary!

Up on the Housetop

After leaving pastoral service, Benjamin Hanby, an Ohioan, wrote this secular carol, which took inspiration from Clement Moore's "Account of a Visit from St. Nicholas," in 1864. The original version didn't have the fourth and fifth verses. When added later, the magazine *Our Song Birds* published the lyrics as below in 1866.

Upon the house, no delay, no pause,
clatter the steeds of Santa Claus;
down thro' the chimney with loads of toys
Ho for the little ones, Christmas joys.

O! O! O! Who wouldn't go,
O! O! O! Who wouldn't go,
upon the housetop, click! click! click!
Down thro' the chimney with good St. Nick.

Look in the stockings of little Will.
Ha! Is it not a "glorious bill"?
Hammer and gimlet and lots of tacks,
Whistle and whirligig, whip that cracks.

O! O! O! Who wouldn't go,
O! O! O! Who wouldn't go,
upon the housetop, click! click! click!
Down thro' the chimney with good St. Nick.

Snow-white stocking of little Nell,
Oh pretty Santa cram it well;
  leave her a dolly that laughs and cries,
  one that can open and shut its eyes.

O! O! O! Who wouldn't go,
O! O! O! Who wouldn't go,
  upon the housetop, click! click! click!
  Down thro' the chimney with good St. Nick.

Here are the stockings of lazy Jim.
What will the good Saint do for him?
  Lo! he is filling them up with bran;
  there, he is adding a new ratan!

O! O! O! Who wouldn't go,
O! O! O! Who wouldn't go,
  upon the housetop, click! click! click!
  Down thro' the chimney with good St. Nick.

Pa, Ma, and Uncle, and Grandma, too,
all I declare have something new;
  even the baby enjoys his part,
  shaking a rattle; now bless his heart.

O! O! O! Who wouldn't go,
O! O! O! Who wouldn't go,
  upon the housetop, click! click! click!
  Down thro' the chimney with good St. Nick.

continues ⟪⟫-

Rover come here; are you all alone?
Haven't they tossed you an extra bone?
  Here's one to gladden your honest jaws;
  now wag a "thank'ee" to Santa Claus.

O! O! O! Who wouldn't go,
O! O! O! Who wouldn't go,
  upon the housetop, click! click! click!
  Down thro' the chimney with good St. Nick.

O Little Town of Bethlehem

After visiting Bethlehem in Palestine, Episcopal priest Phillips Brooks wrote these lyrics in 1868. The words go with different tunes: in America, "St. Louis" by Lewis Redner, Brooks's organist; in Britain, Canada, and Ireland, "Forest Green" as gathered by Ralph Vaughan Williams.

O little town of Bethlehem,
    how still we see thee lie!
Above thy deep and dreamless sleep,
    the silent stars go by.
Yet in thy dark streets shineth
    the everlasting light;
the hopes and fears of all the years
    are met in thee tonight.

For Christ is born of Mary;
    and, gathered all above,
while mortals sleep, the angels keep
    their watch of wond'ring love.
O morning stars, together
    proclaim the holy birth,
and praises sing to God the King,
    and peace to men on earth.

How silently, how silently
   the wondrous gift is giv'n!
So God imparts to human hearts
   the blessings of His heav'n.
No ear may hear His coming,
   but in this world of sin,
where meek souls will receive Him still,
   the dear Christ enters in.

O holy Child of Bethlehem,
   descend to us, we pray;
cast out our sin and enter in;
   be born in us today.
We hear the Christmas angels,
   the great glad tidings tell;
O come to us, abide with us,
   our Lord Emmanuel!

In the Bleak Midwinter

A woman poet, Christina Rossetti achieved fame in her own lifetime, a rarity for the age. She wrote several acclaimed collections as well as the long, narrative poem *Goblin Market*, her best-known work. This carol began as the poem "A Christmas Carol," published in 1872. Gustav Holst set it to music in 1906.

In the bleak midwinter, frosty wind made moan,
earth stood hard as iron, water like a stone;
    snow had fallen, snow on snow, snow on snow,
    in the bleak midwinter, long ago.

Our God, Heaven cannot hold Him, nor earth sustain;
Heaven and earth shall flee away when He comes to reign.
    In the bleak midwinter, a stable place sufficed
    the Lord God Almighty, Jesus Christ.

Enough for Him, whom cherubim worship night and day,
breastful of milk and a mangerful of hay;
    enough for Him, whom angels fall before,
    the ox and ass and camel which adore.

Angels and archangels may have gathered there,
cherubim and seraphim thronged the air;
    but His mother only, in her maiden bliss,
    worshipped the beloved with a kiss.

What can I give Him, poor as I am?
If I were a shepherd, I would bring a lamb;
    if I were a wise man, I would do my part;
    yet what I can I give Him: give my heart.

CHRISTMASTIDE

Numerous composers have set this short poem by Christina Rossetti, first published in 1885, to music. People often sing it to "Garton," a traditional Irish tune.

> Love came down at Christmas,
> Love all lovely, Love Divine.
> Love was born at Christmas;
> Star and Angels gave the sign.
> Worship we the Godhead,
> Love Incarnate, Love Divine.
> Worship we our Jesus,
> but wherewith for sacred sign?
> Love shall be our token;
> Love be yours and love be mine;
> Love to God and all men,
> Love for plea and gift and sign.

AWAY IN A MANGER

For such a short song, this popular carol has an unexpected publishing history with many textual variants. Titled "Luther's Cradle Song," the first two verses appeared anonymously in an 1882 issue of the *Christian Cynosure*, an anti–secret society journal published in Chicago. The third verse appeared in *Gabriel's Vineyard Songs*, published a decade later.

Away in a manger, no crib for His bed,
the little Lord Jesus lay down His sweet head.
　The stars in the [bright] sky looked down where He lay,
　the little Lord Jesus, asleep in the hay.

The cattle are lowing; the poor baby wakes,
but little Lord Jesus, no crying He makes.
　I love Thee, Lord Jesus! Look down from the sky
　and stay by my crib watching my lullaby.

Be near me, Lord Jesus; I ask Thee to stay
close by me forever, and love me, I pray.
　Bless all the dear children in Thy tender care
　and take us to Heaven to live with Thee there.

THE YULE LOG.

Acknowledgements

With thanks to Broo Doherty, my agent at DHH Literary Agency; James Jayo, my editor at Countryman Press; and his colleagues Ann Treistman, Maya Goldfarb, Allison Chi, Jess Murphy, Devon Zahn, Zach Polendo, and Devorah Backman.

The following people helped with the process of this book, in one way or another, either by providing sources or by dog-sitting so I could carry out research! Thank you, in alphabetical order, to Drusilla Broderick, Rachel Chitty, Helen Dawson, Ruth Downes, Jane Monk, Damien Moore, Debby Murphy, Beverley Newton, Jeremy Seal, and William Scheckel.

Index

Page numbers in *italics* refer to illustrations.